The Fundamentals of
iOS 8
With iPad

Kevin Wilson

The Fundamentals of iOS 8: With iPad

Copyright © 2014 Luminescent Media

This work is subject to copyright. All rights are reserved by the Publisher, whether the whole or part of the material is concerned, specifically the rights of translation, reprinting, reuse of illustrations, recitation, broadcasting, reproduction on microfilms or in any other physical way, and transmission or information storage and retrieval, electronic adaptation, computer software, or by similar or dissimilar methodology now known or hereafter developed. Exempted from this legal reservation are brief excerpts in connection with reviews or scholarly analysis or material supplied specifically for the purpose of being entered and executed on a computer system, for exclusive use by the purchaser of the work. Duplication of this publication or parts thereof is permitted only under the provisions of the Copyright Law of the Publisher's location, in its current version, and permission for use must always be obtained from the Publisher. Permissions for use may be obtained through Rights Link at the Copyright Clearance Center. Violations are liable to prosecution under the respective Copyright Law.

Trademarked names, logos, and images may appear in this book. Rather than use a trademark symbol with every occurrence of a trademarked name, logo, or image we use the names, logos, and images only in an editorial fashion and to the benefit of the trademark owner, with no intention of infringement of the trademark.

The use in this publication of trade names, trademarks, service marks, and similar terms, even if they are not identified as such, is not to be taken as an expression of opinion as to whether or not they are subject to proprietary rights.

While the advice and information in this book are believed to be true and accurate at the date of publication, neither the authors nor the editors nor the publisher can accept any legal responsibility for any errors or omissions that may be made. The publisher makes no warranty, express or implied, with respect to the material contained herein.

Publisher: Luminescent Media
Director: Kevin Wilson
Lead Editor: Steven Ashmore
Technical Reviewer: Mike Taylor, Robert Ashcroft
Copy Editors: Joanne Taylor, James Marsh
Proof Reader: Linda Holland
Indexer: James Marsh
Cover Designer: Kevin Wilson

eBook versions and licenses are also available for most titles. Any source code or other supplementary materials referenced by the author in this text is available to readers at

www.luminescentmedia.co.uk/resources

For detailed information about how to locate your book's source code, go to

www.luminescentmedia.co.uk/resources

Acknowledgments

Thanks to all the staff at Luminescent Media for their passion, dedication and hardwork in the preparation and production of this book.

To all my friends and family for their continued support and encouragement in all my writing projects.

To all my colleagues, students and testers who took the time to test procedures and offer feedback on the book

Finally thanks to you the reader for choosing this book. I hope it helps you to use your computer with greater ease.

About the Author

Kevin Wilson, a practicing computer engineer and tutor, has had a passion for gadgets, cameras, computers and technology for many years.

After graduating with masters in computer science, software engineering & multimedia systems, he has worked in the computer industry supporting and working with many different types of computer systems, worked in education running specialist lessons on film making and visual effects for young people. He has also worked as an IT Tutor, has taught in colleges in South Africa and as a tutor for adult education in England.

His books were written in the hope that it will help people to use their computer with greater understanding, productivity and efficiency. To help students and people in countries like South Africa who have never used a computer before. It is his hope that they will get the same benefits from computer technology as we do.

Table of Contents

Setting up your iPad 10
    Initial Setup 11
    Connecting your iPad to a Mac/PC 17
    Using iTunes 18
        Synching your iPad with your Mac/PC 19
    Connecting to the Internet 20
        Wi-Fi 20

Getting to Know IOS 8 22
    New Features 23
        Photos and Camera 23
        Notification Center 24
        Messages 25
        Interface Design 26
        Keyboards 26
        Family Sharing 27
        iCloud Drive 27
        Continuity 28
        Wi-Fi Calling 28
        Spotlight 29
        Health 29
        Instant Hotspot 30
        Safari credit card scanning 30
    Multi-touch Gestures 31
        Tap 31
        Drag 32
        Pinch 32
        Swipe 33
        Four Finger Swipe 33
        Notifications 34
        Command Centre 35
        Search 36
    Multitasking 37
    The Keyboard 39

Using your iPad 40
    Using Safari 41
    AirDrop 43
    Using Email 45
    Contacts 48

Calendar (iCal)	50
Photos	52
Maps	54
App Store	56
Music	59
Transferring Music from your Computer	61
Taking Notes	64
FaceTime	67
Taking Pictures	70
Siri	74
Voice Dictation	75
Arranging Icons	76

Installing iOS 8 78

iOS 8 Settings 82

My Notes & Settings 86

Setting up your iPad

If you've just bought your new iPad and taken it out the box, the process to set it up to use for the first time is very simple. You dont even have to connect it to your computer.

In this section we'll take a look at the processess of setting up your iPad when you turn it on for the first time.

Chapter 1: Setting up your iPad

Initial Setup

To use iPad, you need and internet connection and an Apple ID for some features

Turn iPad on and follow the Setup Assistant. This will guide you through the process

Swipe your finger across the bottom of the screen.

Select Language and Select Country or Region.

Select your Wi-Fi Network. This is where you will need your network key.

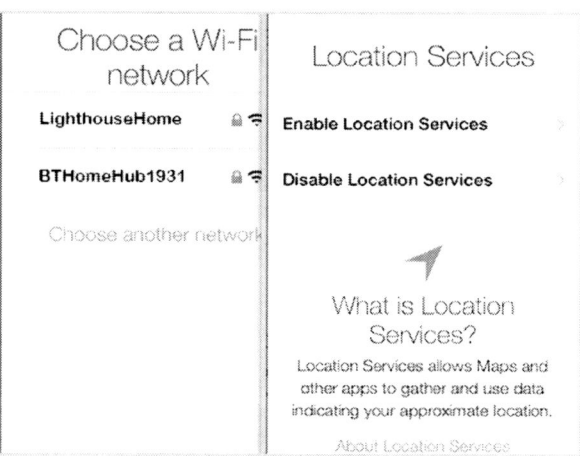

Location Services. The location services allow the iPad to determine your current physical location. Some apps require this, such as maps, etc

Chapter 1: Setting up your iPad

Set up as New iPad.

Tap sign in with your Apple ID, tap sign in with an applie id, enter the username and password. Or create new Apple ID if you don't have one.

Agree to Terms and Conditions. Then Set Up iCloud. Tap use iCloud.

Chapter 1: Setting up your iPad

Tap 'Use Find My iPad'. This is a useful feature if your iPad is lost or stolen and allows you to pinpoint its location.

Tap 'Use Siri'.

Diagnostics. Tap 'don't send'.

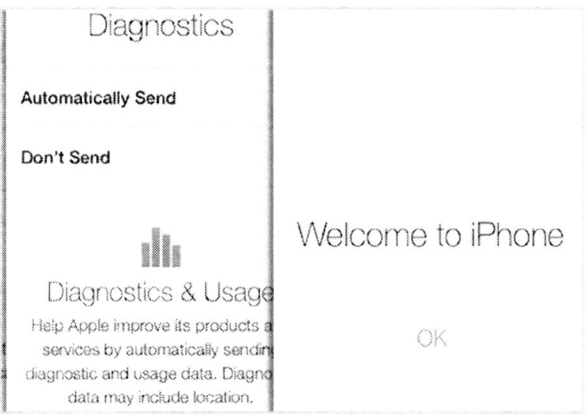

Tap OK to Get Started.

Chapter 1: Setting up your iPad

When you sign into your iPad you will see the home screen.

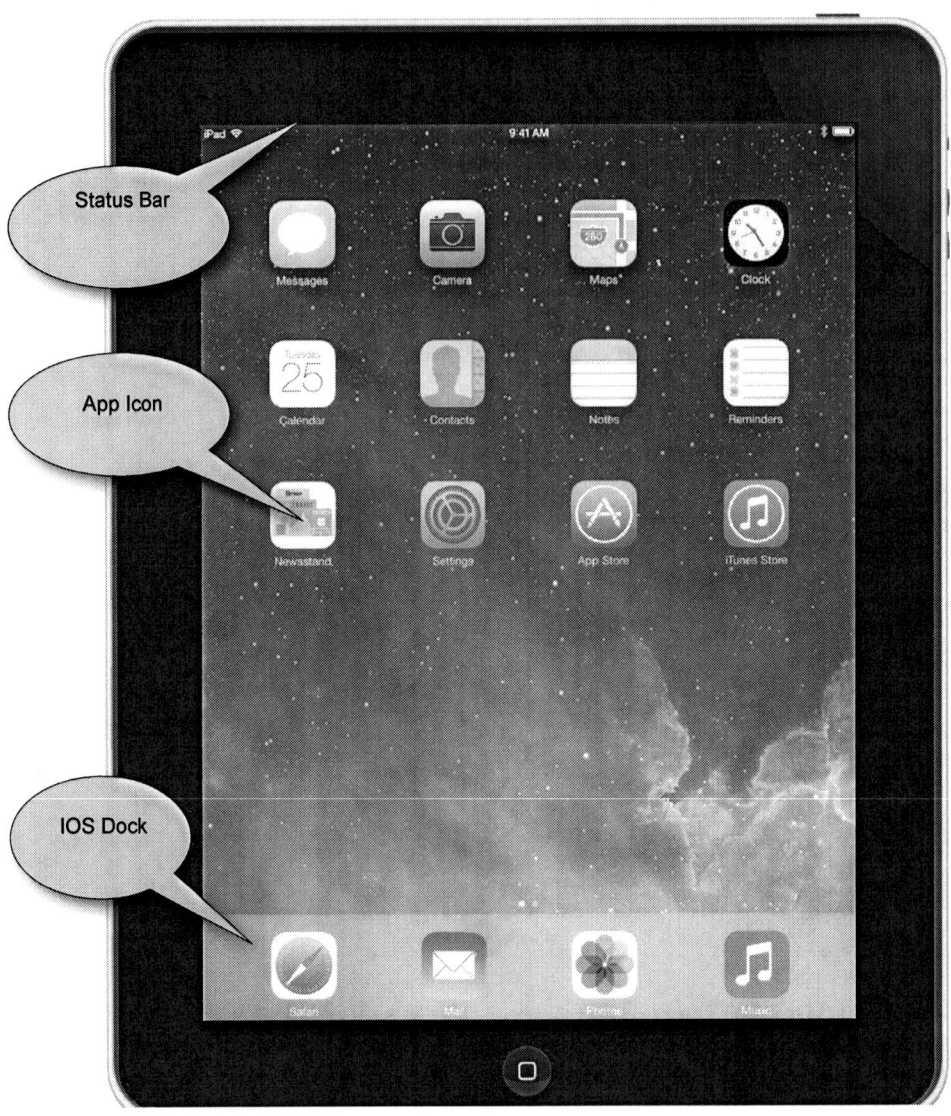

The home screen has a status bar at the top that displays current networks (cellular or wifi etc) and services on the left. In the centre is a clock that displays local time. On the right hand side is a battery indicator .

In the centre of the screen are icons of the apps that are currently installed on the iPad. Some are on already but many can be downloaded from the app store.

Along the bottom of the screen is the Dock. These are the 4 most used apps such as web browsing, email, photos, and music. Might also be phone, mail, safari or music on an iPhone.

Chapter 1: Setting up your iPad

Here is the front of a typical iPad. Note some icons have been enlarged to make it clearer and easier to read in printed form.

Here we have the home button, whenever you want to get back to the home screen from any app, just press this button

Chapter 1: Setting up your iPad

This diagram shows the rear, showing volume controls, speakes and dock connectors etc.

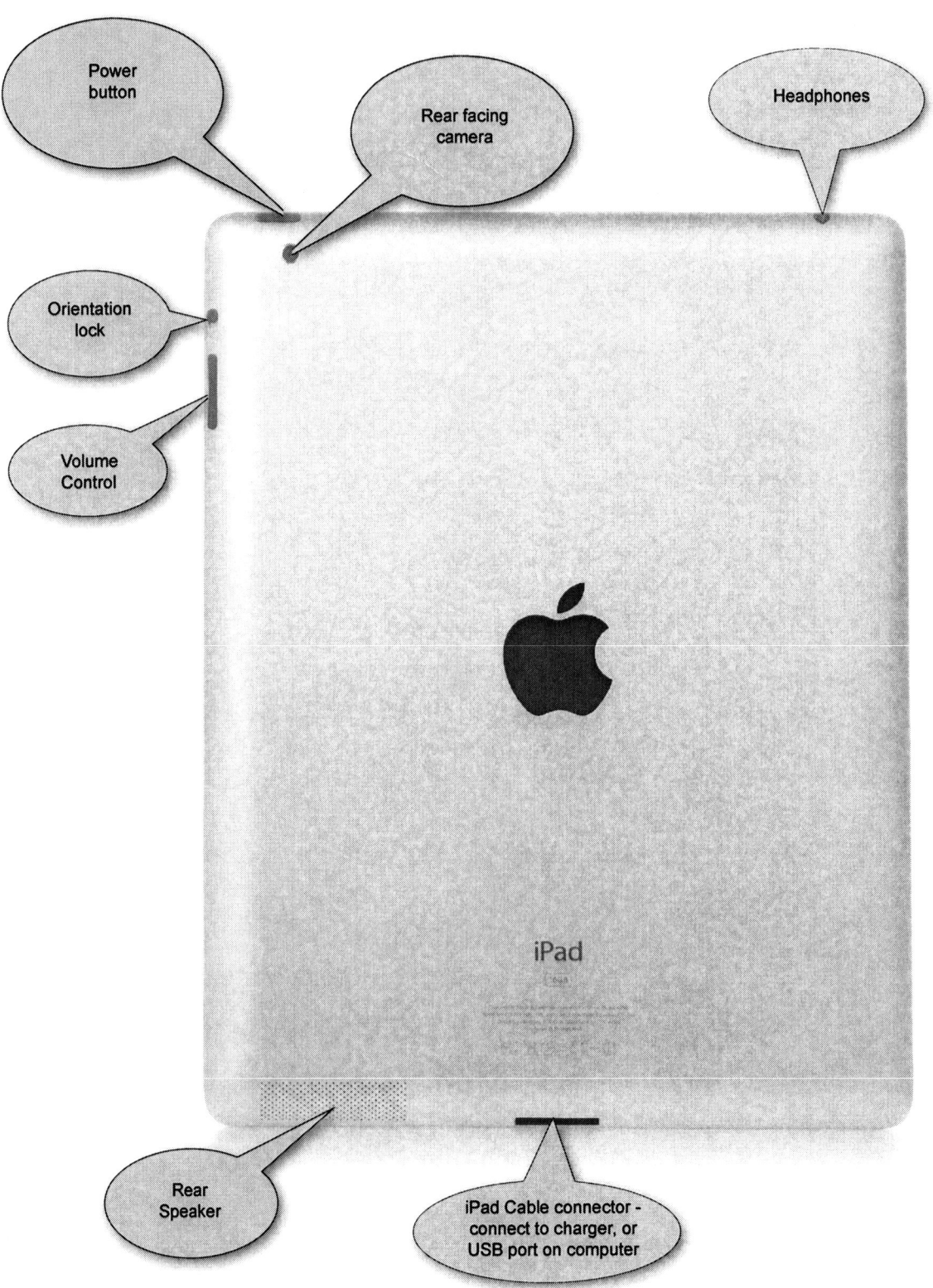

Chapter 1: Setting up your iPad

Connecting your iPad to a Mac/PC

Your iPad cable connects to the underside of your iPad.

The other end of the cable can be plugged into a PC or Mac to allow you to load on music, photos, apps etc.

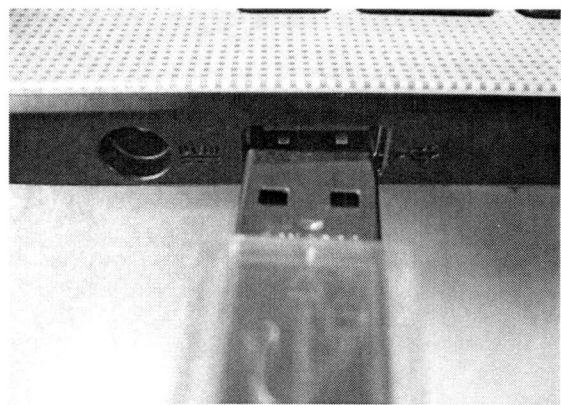

Or it can be plugged into the charger directly to charge up your battery without having to go through a computer.

17

Chapter 1: Setting up your iPad

Using iTunes

To access your iPad from a computer you will need to have iTunes software installed on your computer/mac

You can download it from

`www.apple.com/itunes`

On iTunes' website, click the download link on the top right. Then on the next page remove the ticks from the two boxes shown below right.

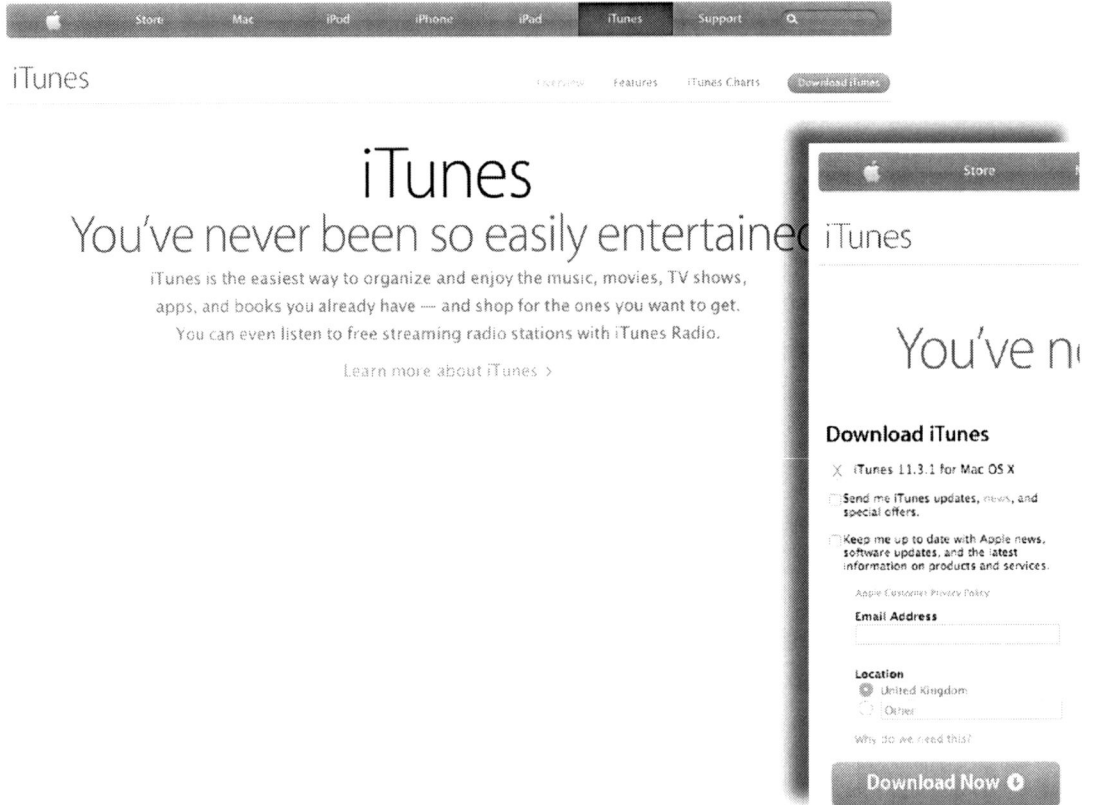

If you want apple to send you lots of notifications via email, enter email address. Otherwise leave it blank.

Click the download now button.

Chapter 1: Setting up your iPad

Synching your iPad with your Mac/PC

Plug your iPad into your computer, iTunes will take a few moments to recognise your device.

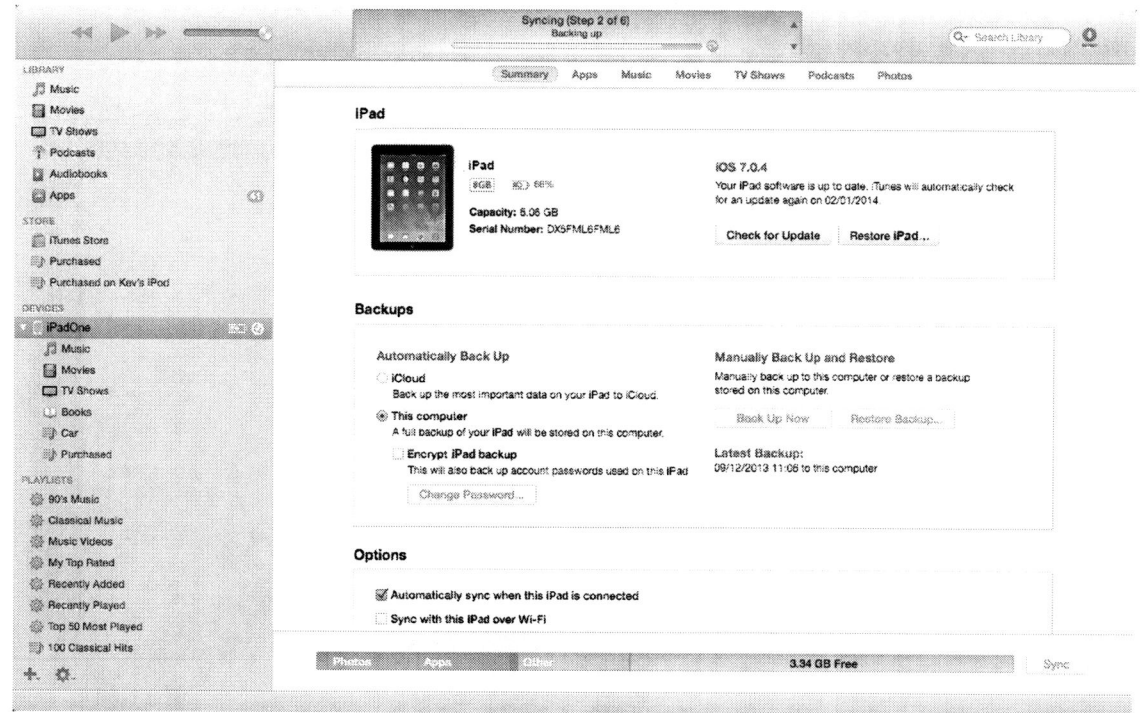

Chapter 1: Setting up your iPad

Connecting to the Internet
Wi-Fi

Wi-Fi is often faster than cellular data networks, but may not be available in many locations.

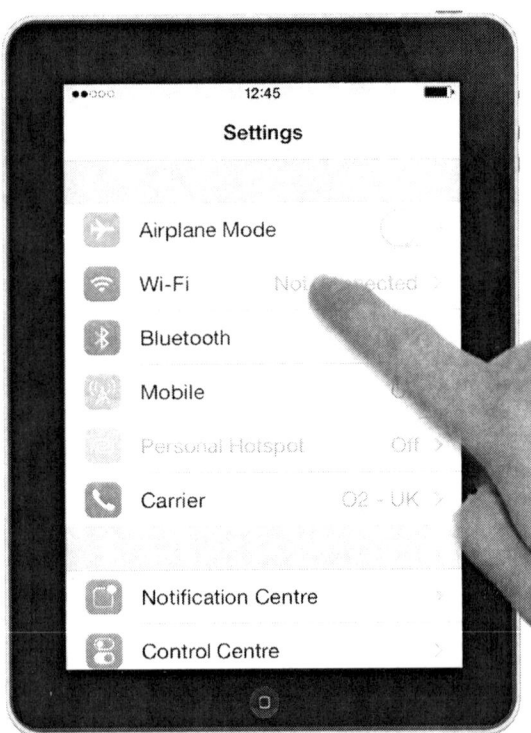 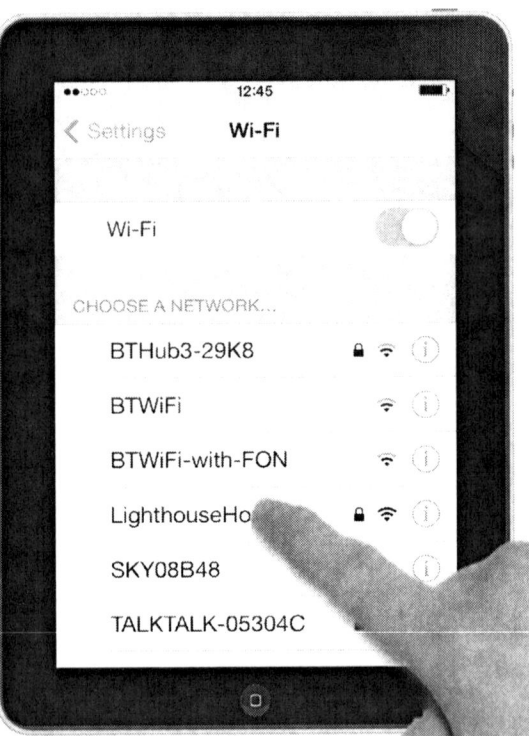

To locate nearby Wi-Fi networks, tap Settings on your home screen.

Tap Wi-Fi, then tap the name of the network you want to join

Enter the wifi password or network key.

Once you have done that tap Join.

The network key or password is usually printed on the back of your router.

Chapter 1: Setting up your iPad

Chapter 2: Getting to Know IOS 8

IOS 8 is the eighth major release of the mobile operating system for iPads, iPods and iPhones

At the time of writing, IOS 8 will be available for the following devices.

- iPhone 4S
- iPhone 5
- iPhone 5C
- iPhone 5S
- iPod Touch (5th generation)
- iPad 2
- iPad (3rd generation)
- iPad (4th generation)
- iPad Air
- iPad Mini (1st generation)
- iPad Mini (2nd generation)
- As well as the new generation of devices

Chapter 2: Getting to Know IOS 8

New Features

IOS 8 introduces a few new features from previous versions.

Photos and Camera

You can now do more to edit and enhance your photos than before. You can rotate images both clockwise and counter-clockwise as well as cropping the image. You can enhance your photos by adjusting brightness and colours.

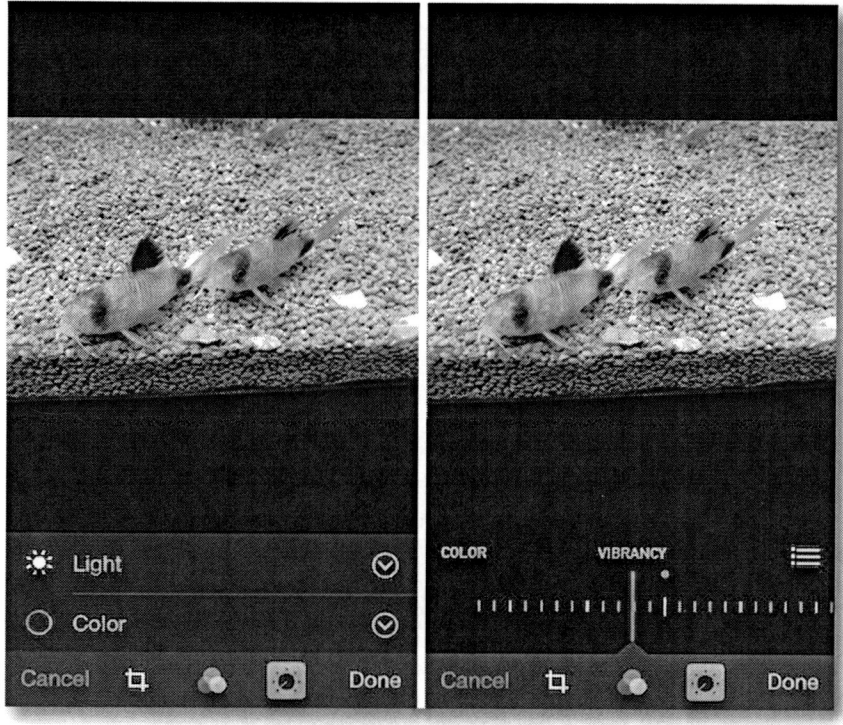

The camera app now features a timer delay, which can be set to 3 or 10 seconds.

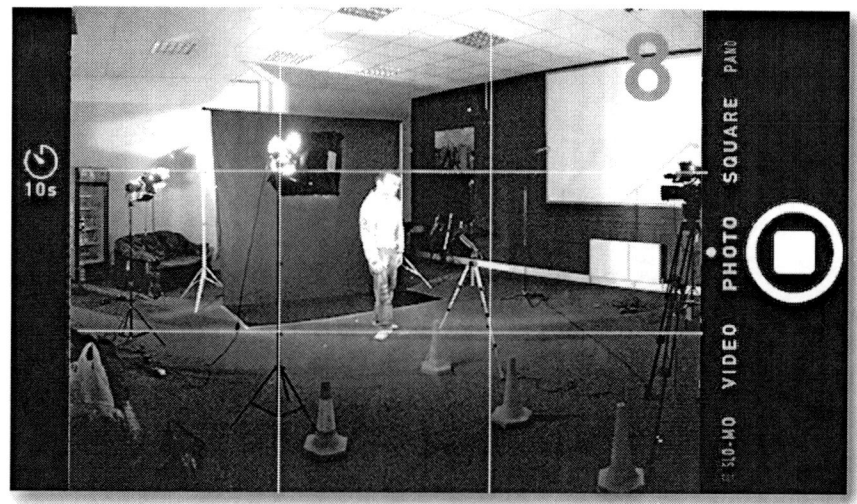

Chapter 2: Getting to Know IOS 8

As well as timelapse and slow motion videos

Notification Center

You can now add and remove widgets in Notification Center with the "Edit" button. This also allows you to rearrange notification widgets.

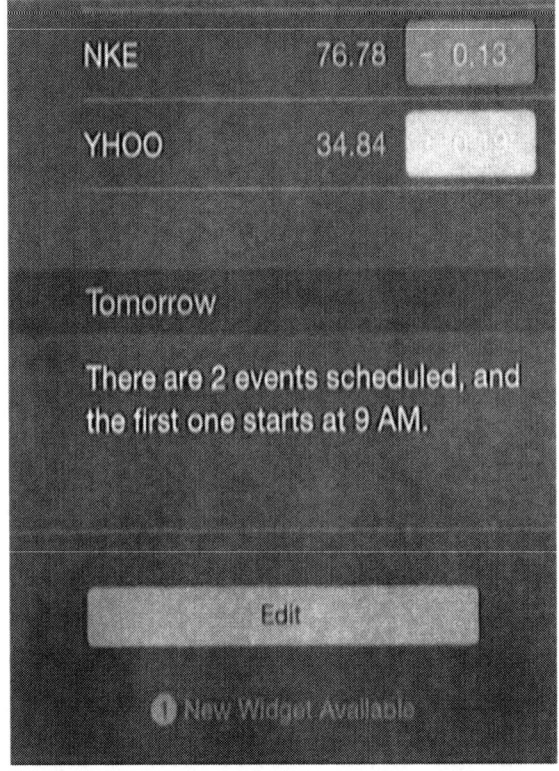

Chapter 2: Getting to Know IOS 8

Messages

You can now send audio and video messages.

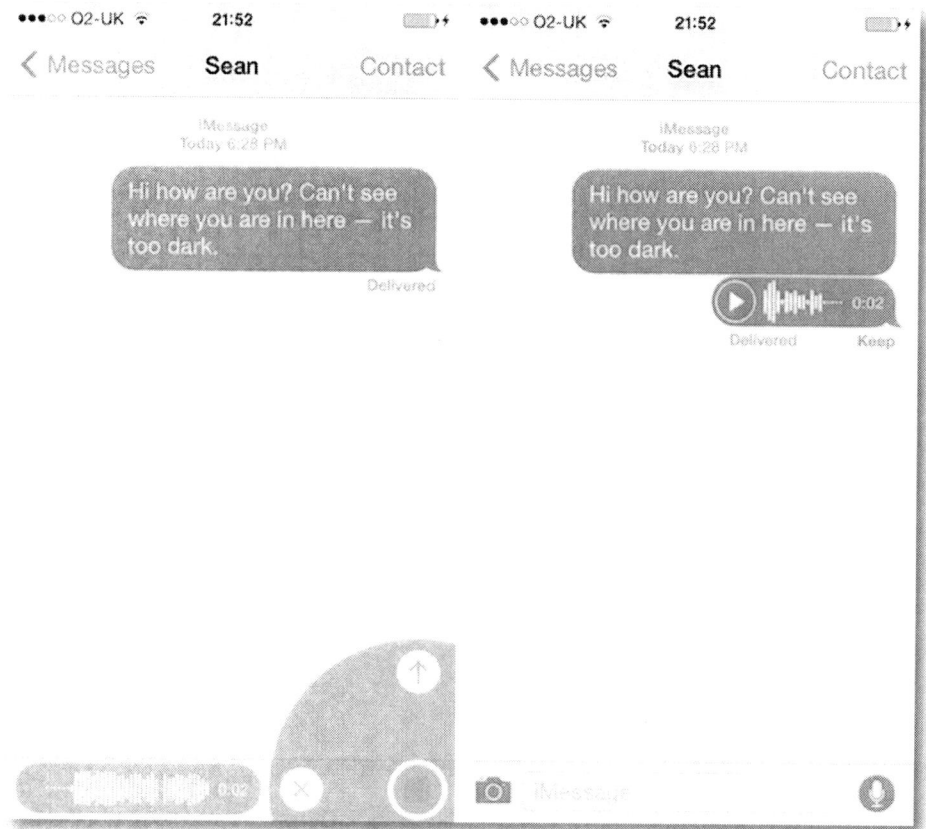

In group conversations, users can add or remove someone from a thread, name a thread, share their location in a thread, view all attachments, and turn on Do Not Disturb to not receive notifications from a specific thread.

Chapter 2: Getting to Know IOS 8

Interface Design

The interface is much the same as its predecessor however there are some improvements. Transparency and other effects have been added.

The multitasking screen now shows a list of recently called and favourite contacts.

Keyboards

iOS 8 now includes a predictive typing feature called QuickType. It displays word selections above the keyboard as you type.

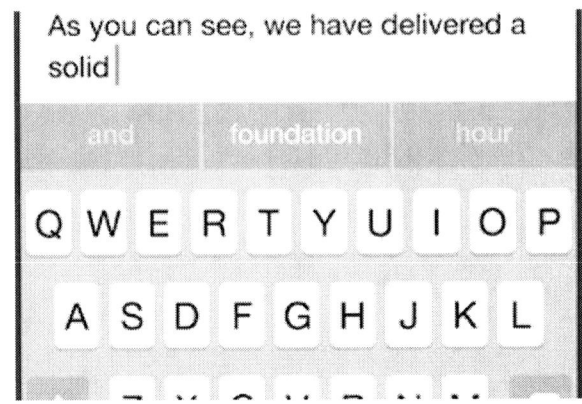

Additionally, you can install third-party keyboards such as emoji and swype.

Chapter 2: Getting to Know IOS 8

Family Sharing

You can now add six others users as family members.

Family members can share purchased apps, music, and books using the same credit card. iOS 8 can also automatically set up photo streams for all family members. Calendars may be synced between all members.

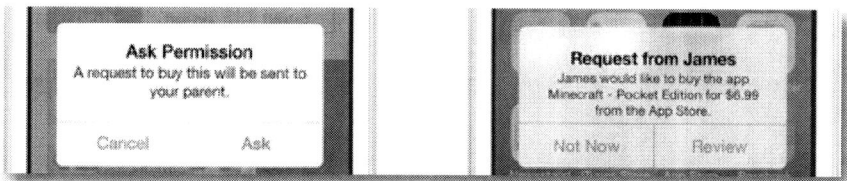

Kids can also send iTunes download requests for apps, music, movies, and more to their parents provided this service is set up correctly.

iCloud Drive

This feature allows users to save photos, videos, documents (Keynote, Pages, and Numbers), and music, and other apps' data to iCloud.

Chapter 2: Getting to Know IOS 8

Users can start their work on one device and continue on another device and will get 5 gigabytes of storage for free

Continuity

Continuity allows users to share documents, e-mails, and websites over Wi-Fi to iOS 8 and OS X Yosemite devices. For example, when you're working on an email, Pages document, Keynote presentation, Numbers spreadsheet, viewing a location in Maps or if you're browsing Safari on your Mac, on the lock screen of your iOS device it shows you what app you're currently using on your Mac and will allow you to pick up where you left off in that app you were using on your Mac.

Continuity also allows users to reply to SMS messages and answer phone calls on their Mac or iPad if they own an iPhone. This feature is supported only by compatible Macs running OS X Yosemite, or by devices running iOS 8.

Wi-Fi Calling

This service allows mobile phone calls over Wi-Fi.

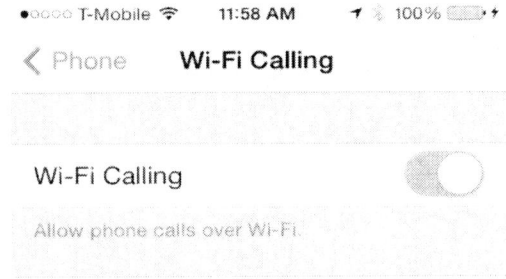

Chapter 2: Getting to Know IOS 8

Spotlight

Spotlight is integrated with a number of web services so that users can search using Wikipedia, Bing, or Google. Other services include: news, nearby places, suggested websites, movie showtimes, and content that is not already on the device from the iTunes Store

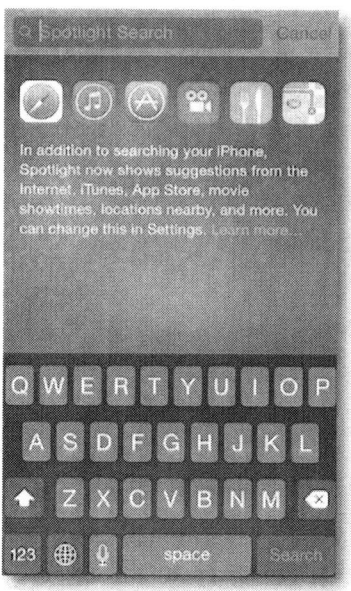

Health

Something which was highly anticipated for iOS 8 was Apple's own health app. It includes sections for Diagnostics, Fitness, Lab Results, Medications, Nutrition, Sleep, Vitals, and more, along with an Emergency Card displaying medical conditions and allergies.

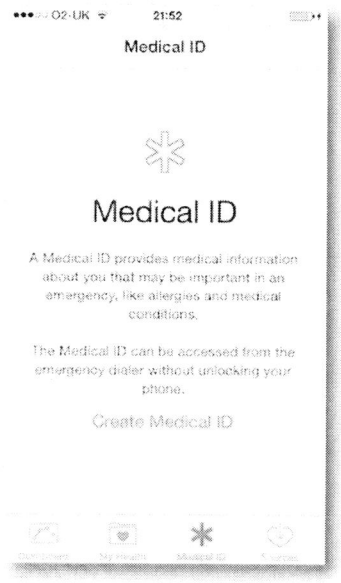

29

Chapter 2: Getting to Know IOS 8

Instant Hotspot

When the iPhone is near your Mac it will auto-connect to the iPhone for connectivity.

Safari credit card scanning

Safari can utilize the camera to scan in credit card numbers when making online purchases, a faster alternative than manually entering a credit card number. Currently, this scanning function is available in the App Store to scan in iTunes Cards, and the credit card scan functions in the same way.

Chapter 2: Getting to Know IOS 8

Multi-touch Gestures

Gestures, sometimes called multi-touch gestures, are what you'll use to interact with the touch screen on iPad. All it takes is the touch of a finger to use your favourite apps, navigate the web, and access all the things you need.

Tap

Tap your index finger on an icon or select something on the screen.

For example, you can tap on an app icon, a link in safari or even a song you want to download.

You can also tap and hold your finger on the screen to access other options that might be available (this is like right-clicking the mouse on your computer).

31

Chapter 2: Getting to Know IOS 8

Drag

Tap on the screen and without lifting your finger off run your finger across to drag up and down, left or right, or any other direction on the screen.

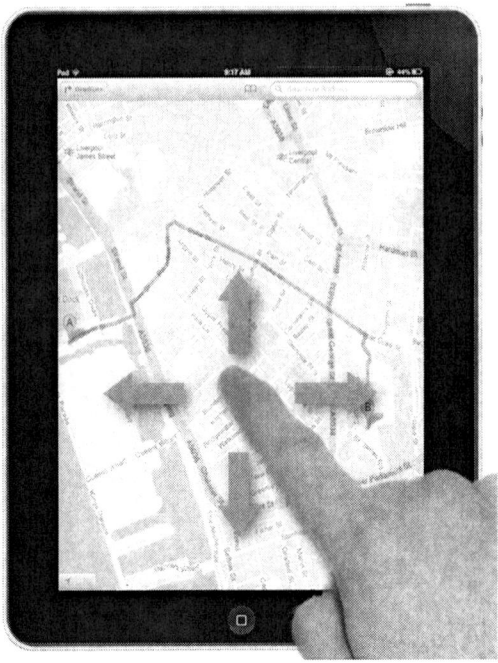

Pinch

Hold your index finger and thumb on the area you want to zoom in on and pinch the screen to zoom in or out almost anywhere.

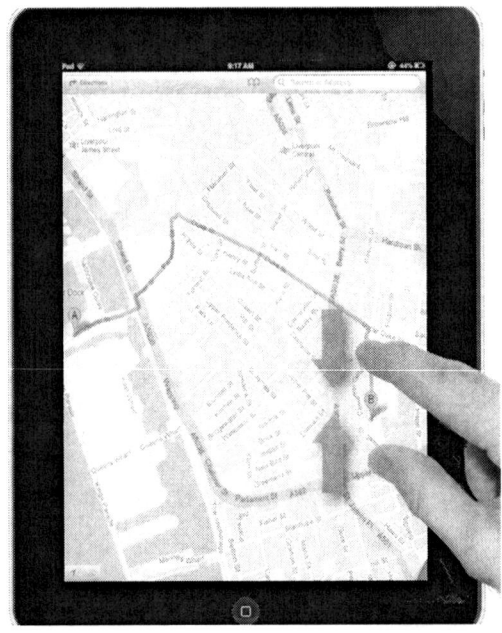

Chapter 2: Getting to Know IOS 8

Swipe

This allows you to flip through photos, pages in an e-book, pages on the home screen, etc. You swipe almost like striking a match.

Four Finger Swipe

Hold your four fingers (not your thumb) on the screen and swipe across to switch between open apps.

Chapter 2: Getting to Know IOS 8

Notifications

Swipe your finger downwards from the top edge of the screen to reveal the notifications centre. This is where you can find your calendars to see appointments or reminders

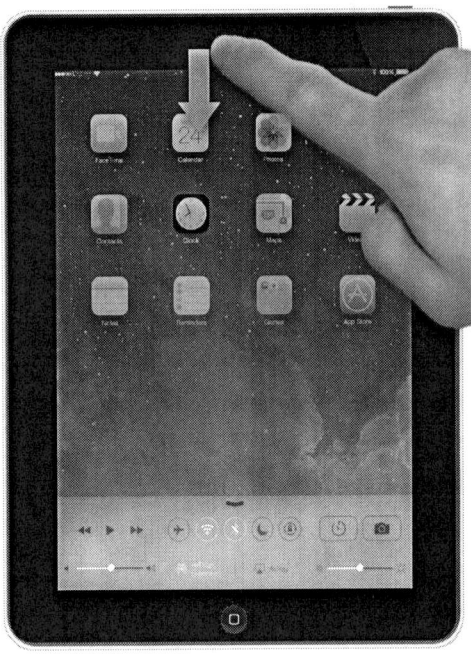 

Chapter 2: Getting to Know IOS 8

Command Centre

Swipe your finger upwards from the bottom edge of the screen.

This reveals the command centre where you can control the volume of playing music, turn on and off wifi, bluetooth, access your camera, set the orientation lock to stop the screen shifting - this can be useful if you are reading a book etc.

Main Volume Control

Screen Brightness Control

35

Chapter 2: Getting to Know IOS 8

Search

To activate spotlight search, swipe your finger down from the centre of the screen.

The search box will appear at the top of the screen. Tap inside the search field and type your words in the keyboard that appears.

Chapter 2: Getting to Know IOS 8

Multitasking

iOS is called a multitasking operating system. This means that you can run more than one app at a time. Most apps will be running in the background. To quickly see what apps are running, press your home button twice.

You can scroll through the list left and right by swiping your finger across the screen. After time you will find that there are a lot of apps running, this can severely affect the performance of your iPad and drain your battery more quickly. To close apps, swipe your finger upwards on the app you want to close.

37

Chapter 2: Getting to Know IOS 8

You can also use this technique to switch between apps. Press your home button twice, then swipe your finger left and right to browse through the apps, then tap on the app you want to switch to.

Chapter 2: Getting to Know IOS 8

The Keyboard

Typing on an iPad, iPhone or iPod touch is easy using the on-screen Multi-Touch keyboard. Tap in any text field, eg if you are browsing the web and you want to search for something in google.

Once you tap a text field, the keyboard will appear on the bottom of the screen. You can type by tapping on the keys.

By adding the Emoji keyboard configuration via the Settings app it's possible to add one of these symbols at any time.

Tap settings -> Tap General -> Tap Keyboard -> Tap Keyboards - >Tap add new keyboard -> Scroll down, tap Emoji.

# Using your iPad

The iOS on the iPad comes with a number of built in apps such as calendar, photos, camera, clocks, maps, videos, notes, reminders, itunes and app store. As well as facetime, books, safari web browser and email.

You can also download a large number of apps from the app store. There is an app for virtually anything.

In this secion we will look at some of the built in apps and the most commonly used apps from the app store.

Lets begin by having a look at safari web browser.

Chapter 3: Using your iPad

Using Safari

To launch safari, tap on the safari icon located on your dock.

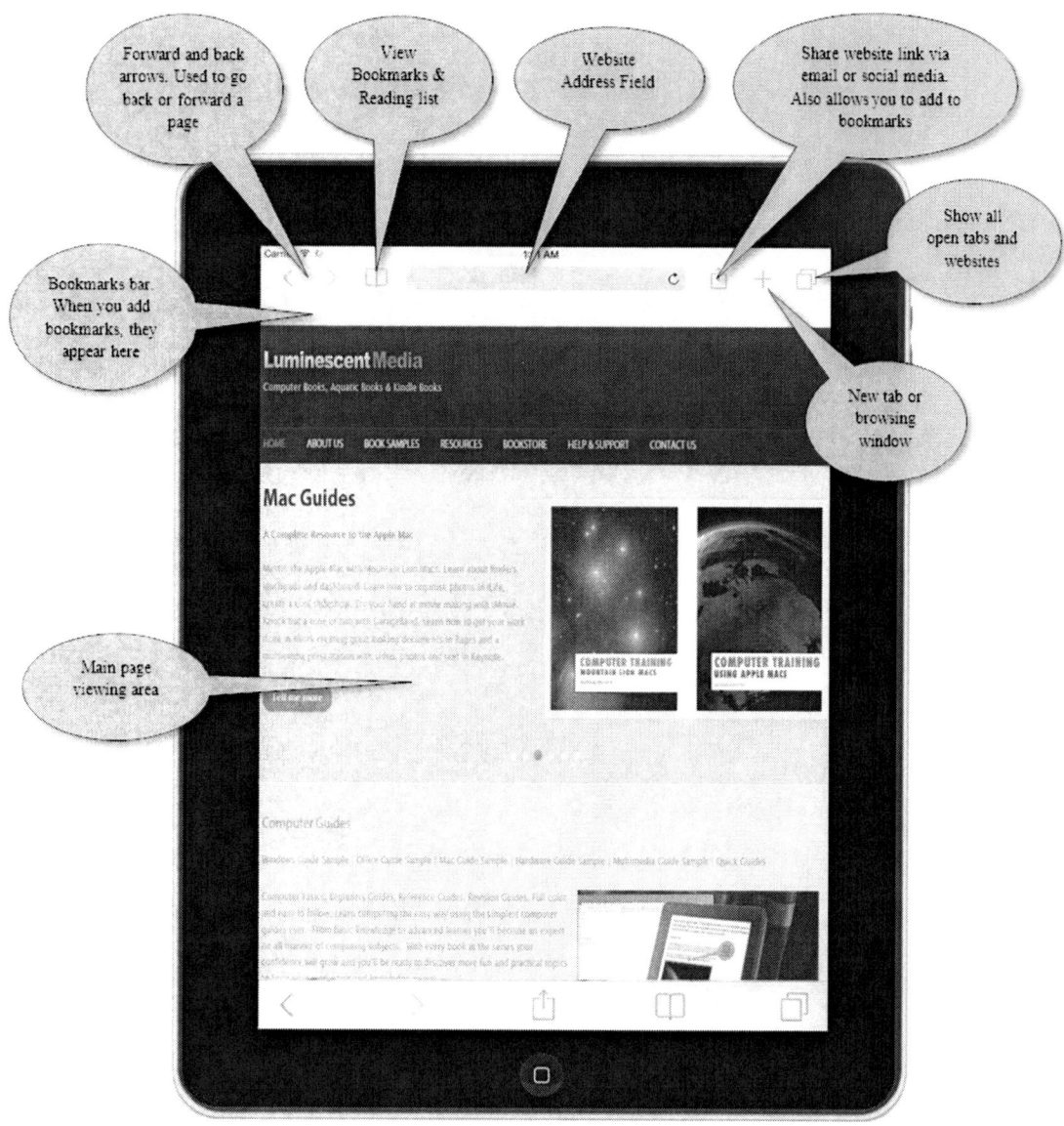

This will launch into safari's main screen.

In safari's main screen, tap in the address field, to enter the website's address, tap in the google search and enter your search.

Two menus to take note of.

Chapter 3: Using your iPad

The first one is on the left hand side of the screen and allows you to access favourite or bookmarked sites.

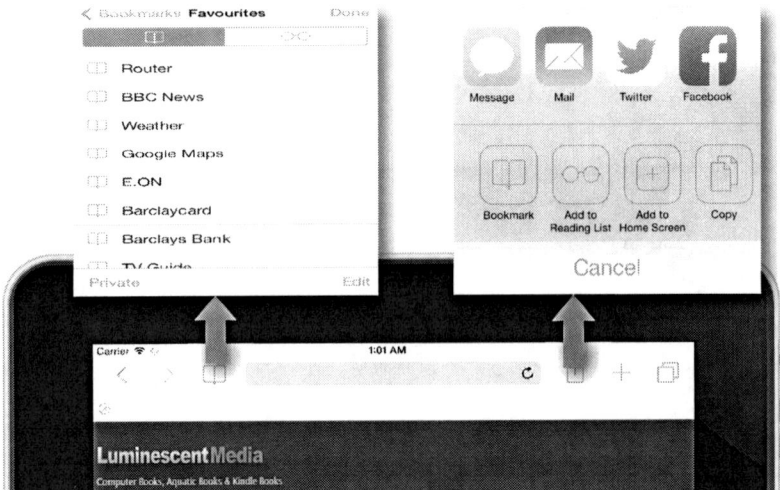

The second, is on the right hand side and allows you to share the current website link via text message, email or social media. Along the bottom of that menu, you can add the current site to bookmarks/favourites.

Chapter 3: Using your iPad

AirDrop

AirDrop allows you to transfer files from one device to another using bluetooth wireless technology.

To use AirDrop you will need a compatible device, such as the iPhone 5 or later, fourth-generation iPad, iPad mini, and fifth-generation iPod touch, and have both Bluetooth and Wi-Fi enabled.

Turn on Wi-Fi and Bluetooth either in Settings or the Control Panel.

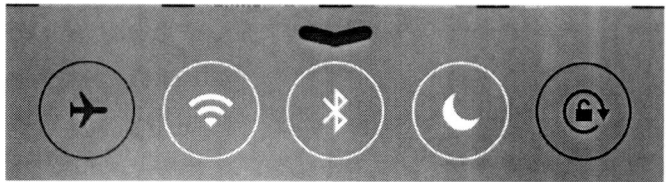

To enable AirDrop open Control Centre and press the AirDrop icon. Make yourself discoverable to just those in your contacts.

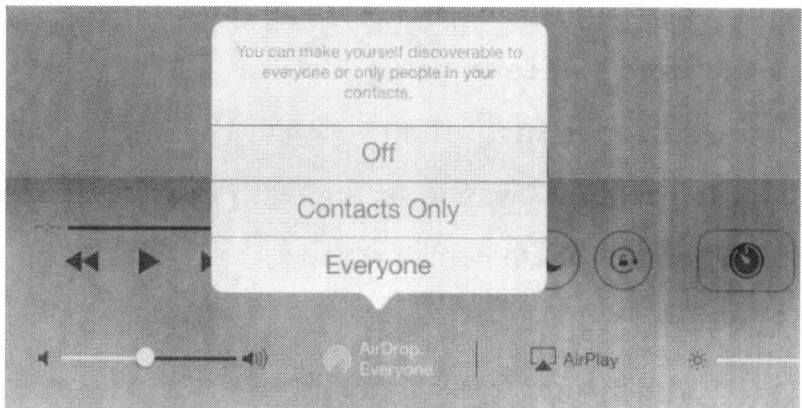

You can send a photo from iphone to another iphone or another ipad.

Launch Photos app.

Tap the image you want to share from your albums, tap next.

Tap on the Share button.

Tap airdrop.

AirDrop will detect other devices in the vicinity.

Chapter 3: Using your iPad

Devices with AirDrop enabled, and on the same Wi-Fi network, will appear listed underneath the selected image as shown below

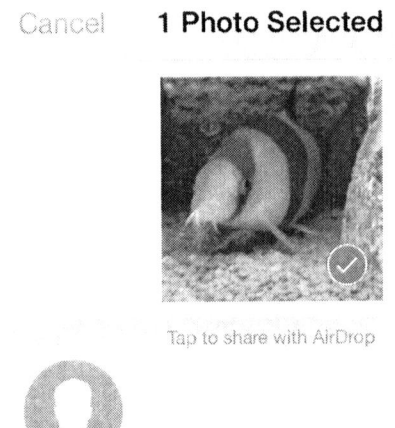

Tap the icon of the person/device you want to send to.

To receive a file from someone using AirDrop

Make sure your AirDrop is enabled on your device.

AirDrop will try to negotiate the connection with near by devices

Tap on Accept when the photo comes through

Go into your photos app and the photo will be stored in there.

Chapter 3: Using your iPad

Using Email

To start the mail app, tap Mail on the bottom of the screen.

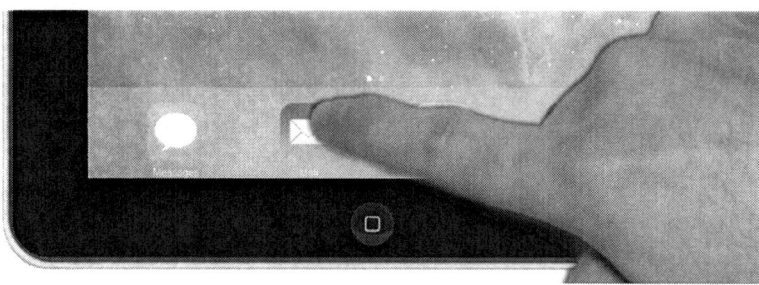

If this is the first time running the mail app, it will ask you to set it up by entering your email account information.

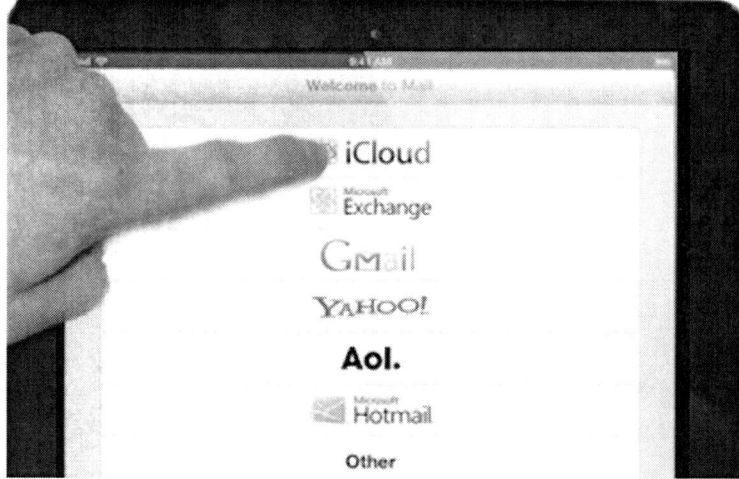

Select the type of account you have, eg hotmail, yahoo, gmail, icloud etc. I have an icloud account so I am going to go ahead and select that one.

Type in your email address and password and click next.

Chapter 3: Using your iPad

Once your email is setup it will open on the main screen. On the left hand side is a list of all your emails. Just tap to view.

To open emails in full, double tap on the message in your list on the left hand side

To reply to an email open the email you want from your inbox then tap reply to email icon

To send a new message click the compose new email icon

Chapter 3: Using your iPad

This will bring up a new email. Tap in the 'To:' field to enter an email address. If you are replying to a message, the email address of the person that sent you the message will appear here automatically.

Tap in the subject field and add some text.

Tap in the message body underneath and type your message using the pop up on screen keyboard.

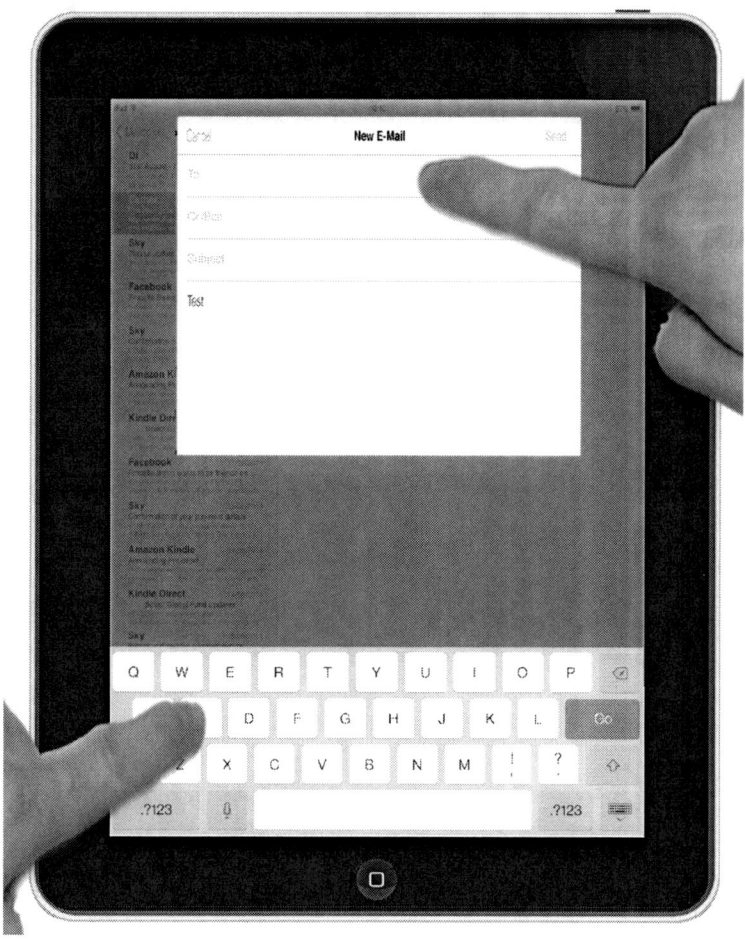

When you have finished, tap send.

Chapter 3: Using your iPad

Contacts

Contacts is your main address book. It contains all the names, email addresses, phone numbers and addresses of the people you correspond with.

Launch address book by tapping on the icon on your home screen

This is the main screen. You can browse contacts, or add new ones.

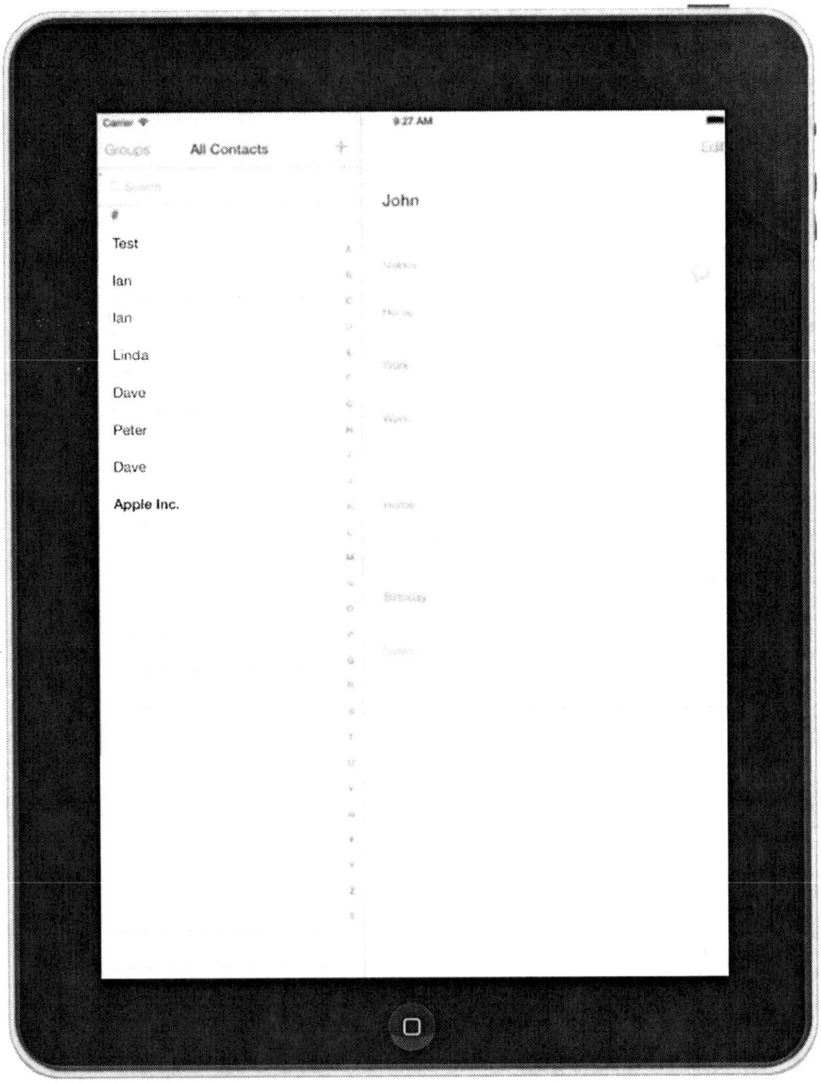

Chapter 3: Using your iPad

Tap on the name, you can send a message, FaceTime them if they have it or give them a call.

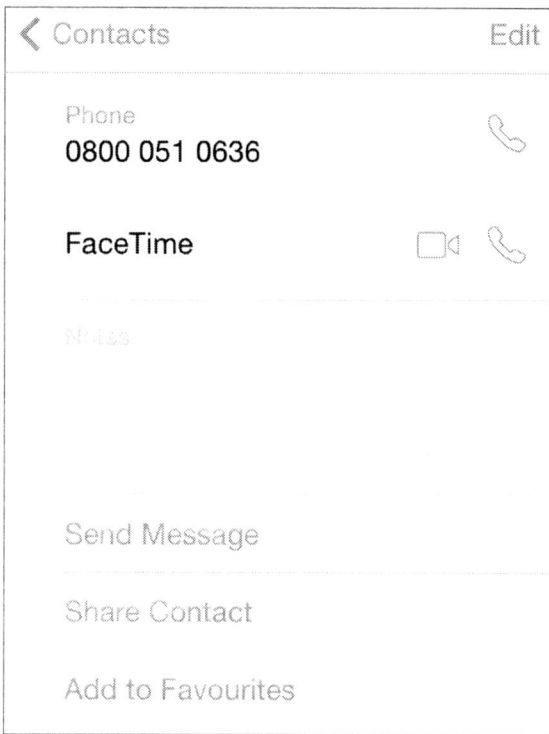

Chapter 3: Using your iPad

Calendar (iCal)

To start calendar app, tap the icon on the main screen

This will bring up the calendar main screen. I found it easiest to view the calendar in month or week view.

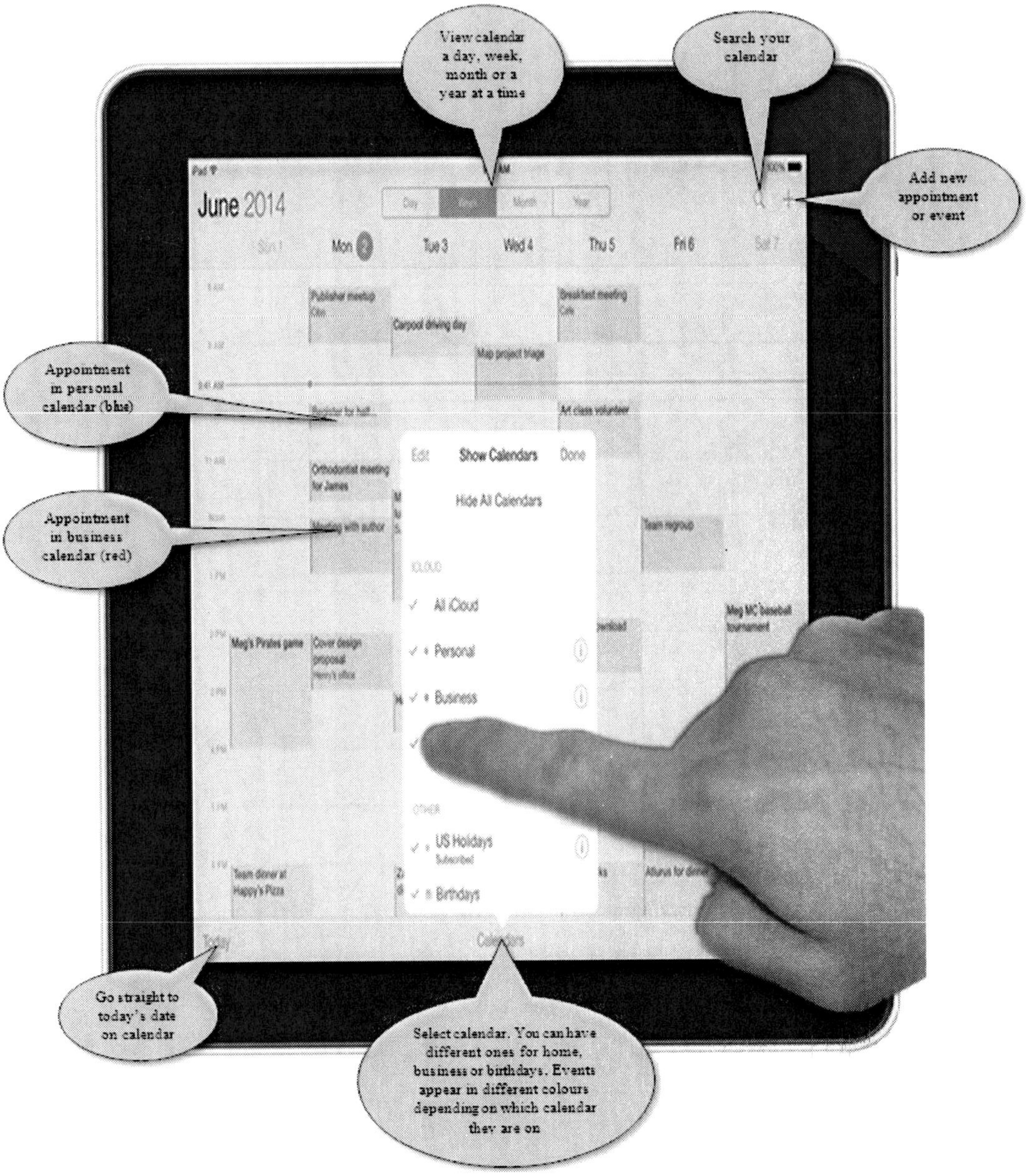

Chapter 3: Using your iPad

To add an event to the calendar, tap and hold your finger on the day the event falls on.

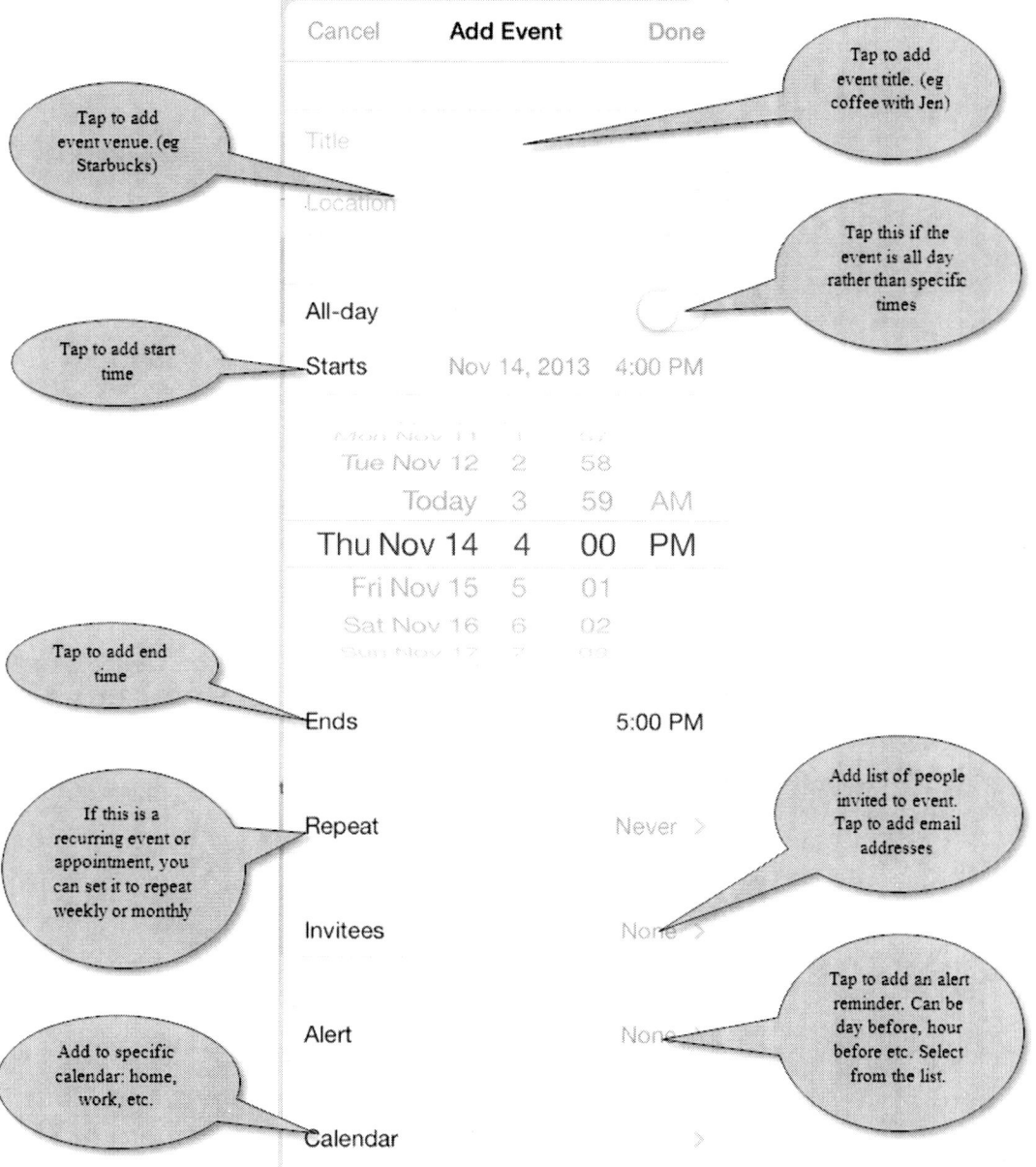

Then fill in the details by tapping them such as title (what the event or appointment is), location, and times. Once you are finished tap done.

51

Chapter 3: Using your iPad

Photos

There are two adapters available to accomplish this: the Lightning to USB Camera Adapter, or the Lightning to SD Card Camera Reader.

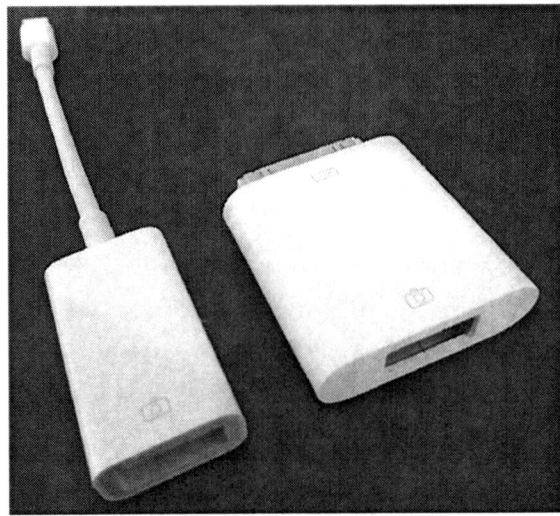

The camera adapter allows you to use a USB cable to transfer photos from your camera straight to your iPad

The card reader enables you to insert the SD card from your camera and copy images from it.

The card reader plugs into the docking port on the bottom of the iPad. Launch the iPhoto app. If it doesn't automatically tap on camera or card.

Chapter 3: Using your iPad

Then tap the photographs you want to import and then tap import to copy the photos across.

Once the photos have been imported, you will be prompted asking you whether to keep the images or delete them. If you select keep, this leaves all the photos intact on the memory card. If you select delete, this deletes the photos you just imported off the memory card.

Chapter 3: Using your iPad

Maps

Maps can be extremely useful if you are trying to find out where a particular place is and need to find driving directions. It works almost like a satnav giving you precise directions straight from door to door.

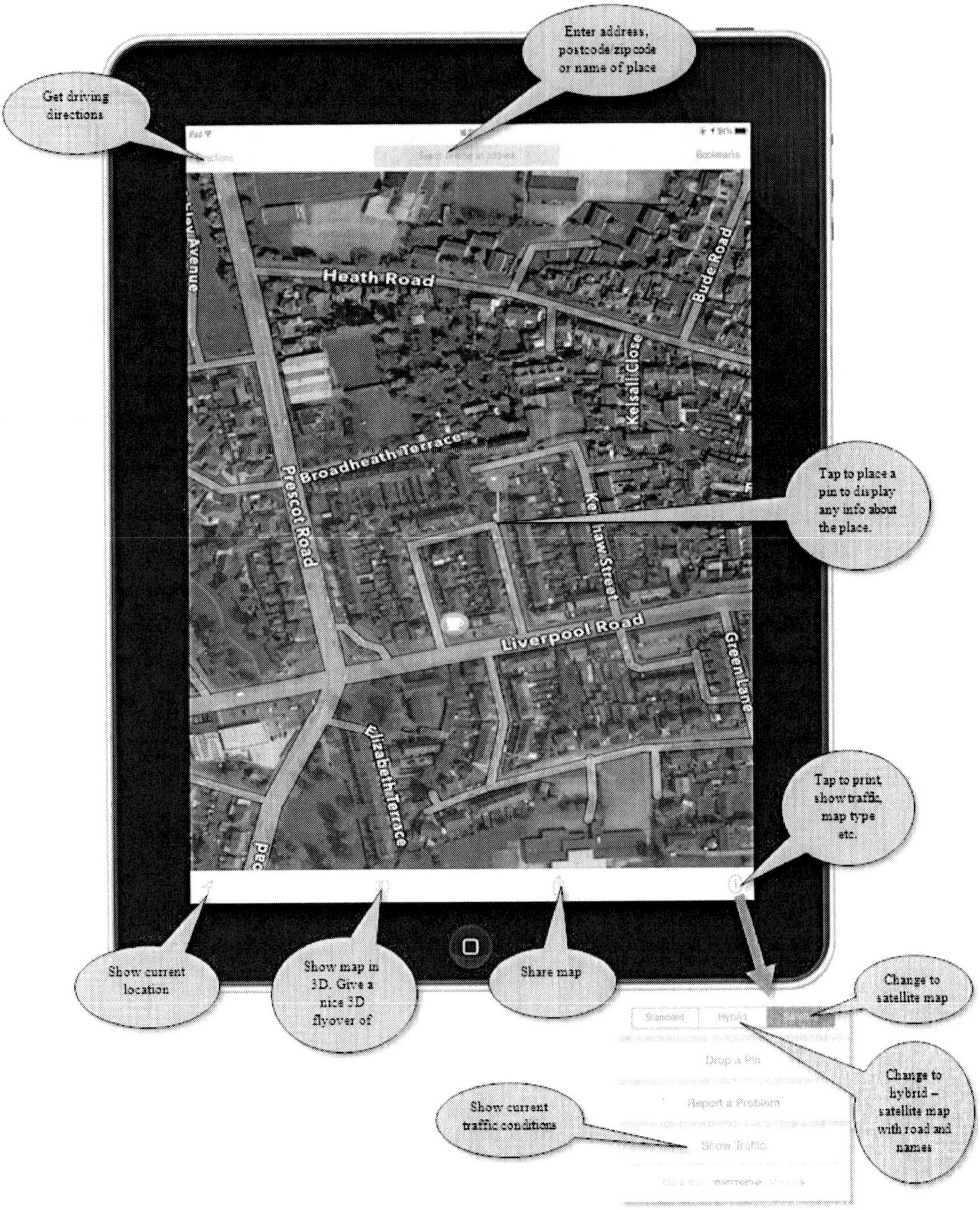

- Get driving directions
- Enter address, postcode/zip code or name of place
- Tap to place a pin to display any info about the place.
- Tap to print, show traffic, map type etc.
- Show current location
- Show map in 3D. Give a nice 3D flyover of
- Share map
- Change to satellite map
- Show current traffic conditions
- Change to hybrid – satellite map with road and names

Chapter 3: Using your iPad

You can find driving directions by tapping the directions icon on the maps main screen. In the menu that appears enter your destination address in the end field. Then tap route when done.

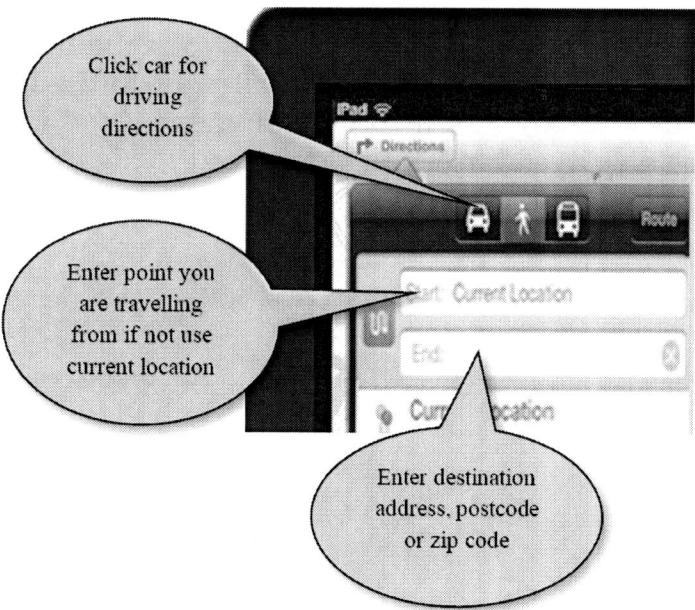

You will see a list of turn by turn directions and your route will he highlighted in blue on the map

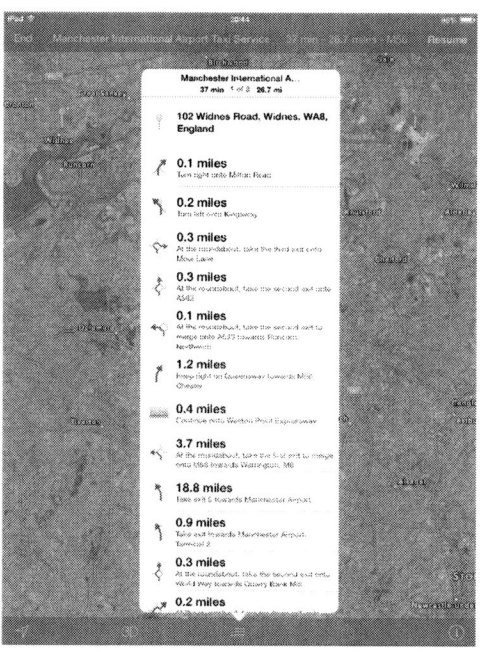

Tapping on resume on the top right, gives you turn by turn directions. Tap screen for next instruction.

Chapter 3: Using your iPad

App Store

The app store has over 300,000 apps available for download direct to your iPad without even going on a computer.

To start app store, click App Store app on your main screen. Once on the app store's main screen, scroll right to the bottom of the page and select sign in. If you are already signed in, your apple id will be displayed here, you won't need to sign in again.

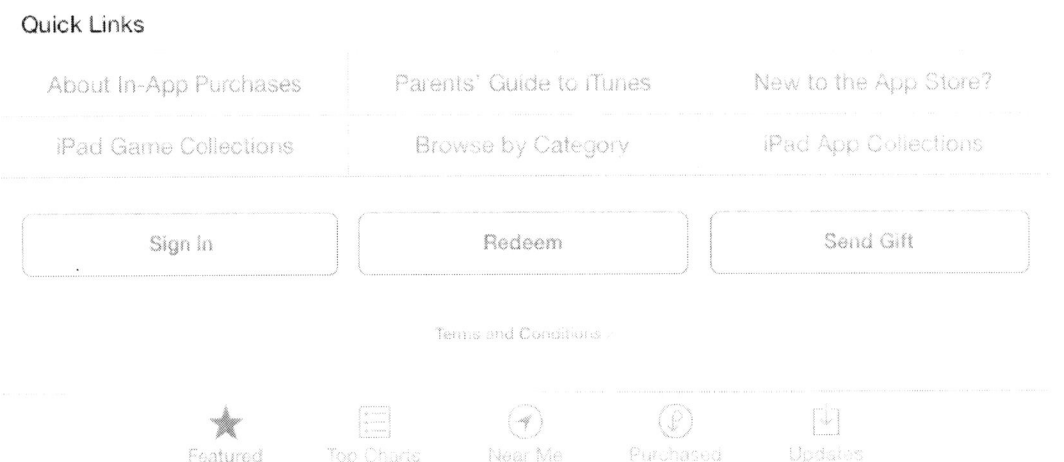

In the box that appears, click use existing apple id, and enter your details

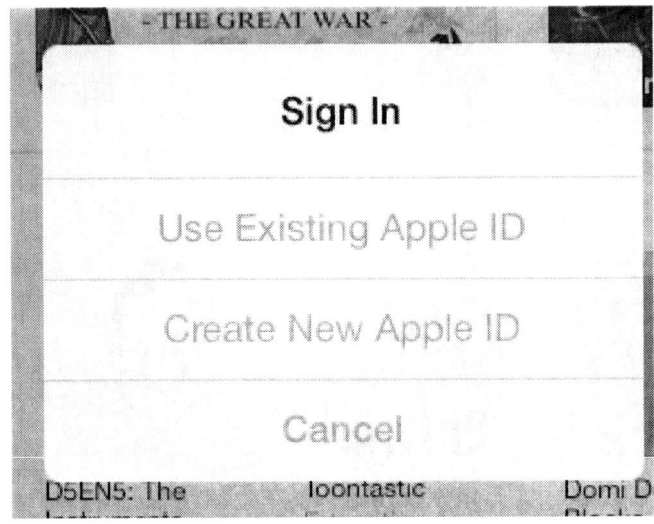

Chapter 3: Using your iPad

On the app store, you will find everything from games and entertainment, productivity tools such as word processing.

You can even find apps for recipes, travel details, maps. There is an app for almost anything you can think of.

Chapter 3: Using your iPad

Just type it into the search on the app store main screen shown below.

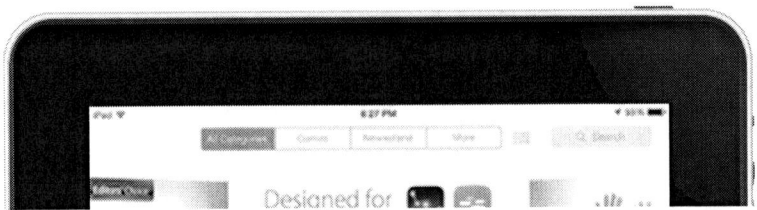

If you are more the browsing type, app store has grouped all the apps into categories according to their use. You can find the categories on the bar at the top of app store's screen.

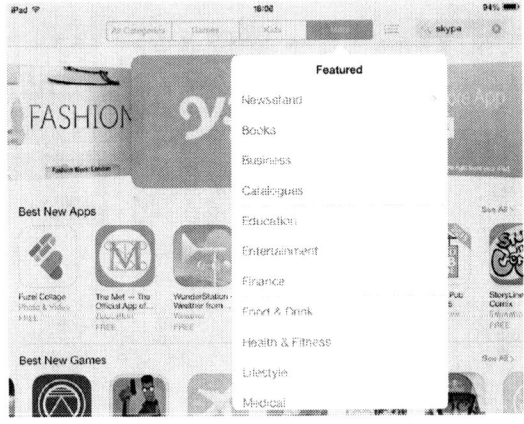

To get more information on the particular app, tap on the app's icon. This gives you information about what the app does, what it costs, some screen shots of the app in action and the device requirements in order to run the app.

To purchase an app just tap on the price tag, then tap the buy icon that appears.

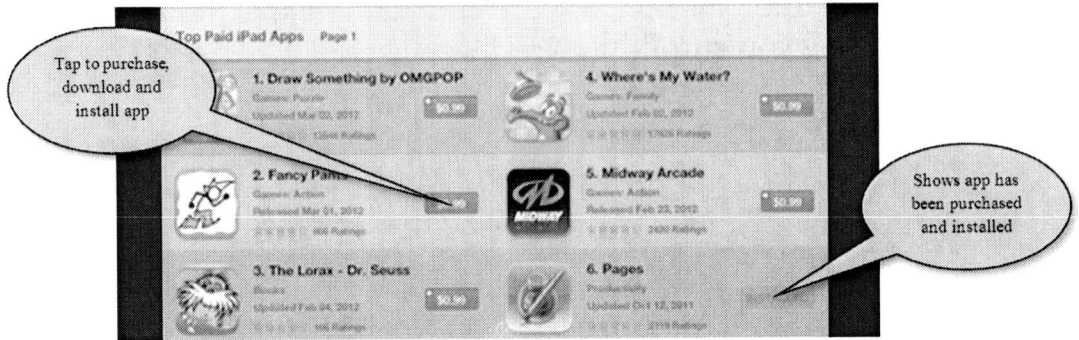

Chapter 3: Using your iPad

Music

You can start the music app by tapping on music icon on the main screen.

Once music app has loaded you can see all the albums that are currently on your iPad

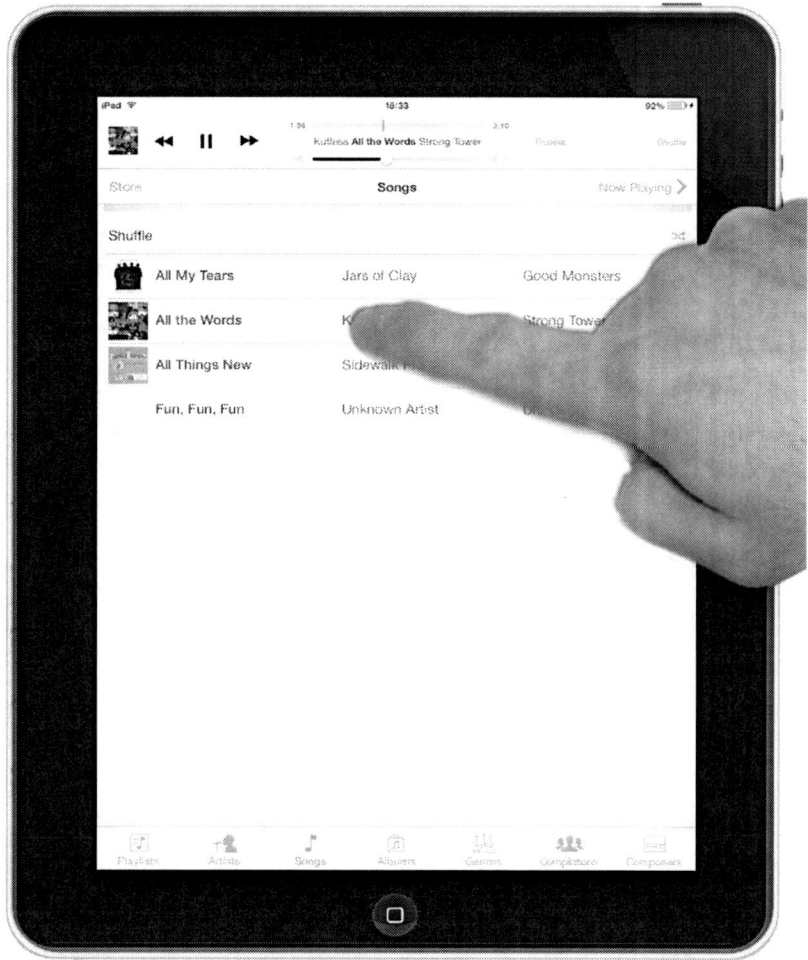

Tapping on the album cover brings up the song list. Just tap the song on the song list and it will start playing. Time to put on your headphones.

Chapter 3: Using your iPad

You can start the iTunes store by tapping on the icon on your home screen

Once the app has loaded you can browse through music, movies and tv shows by tapping on the icons. You can also type what you are looking for in the search field on the top right of the screen.

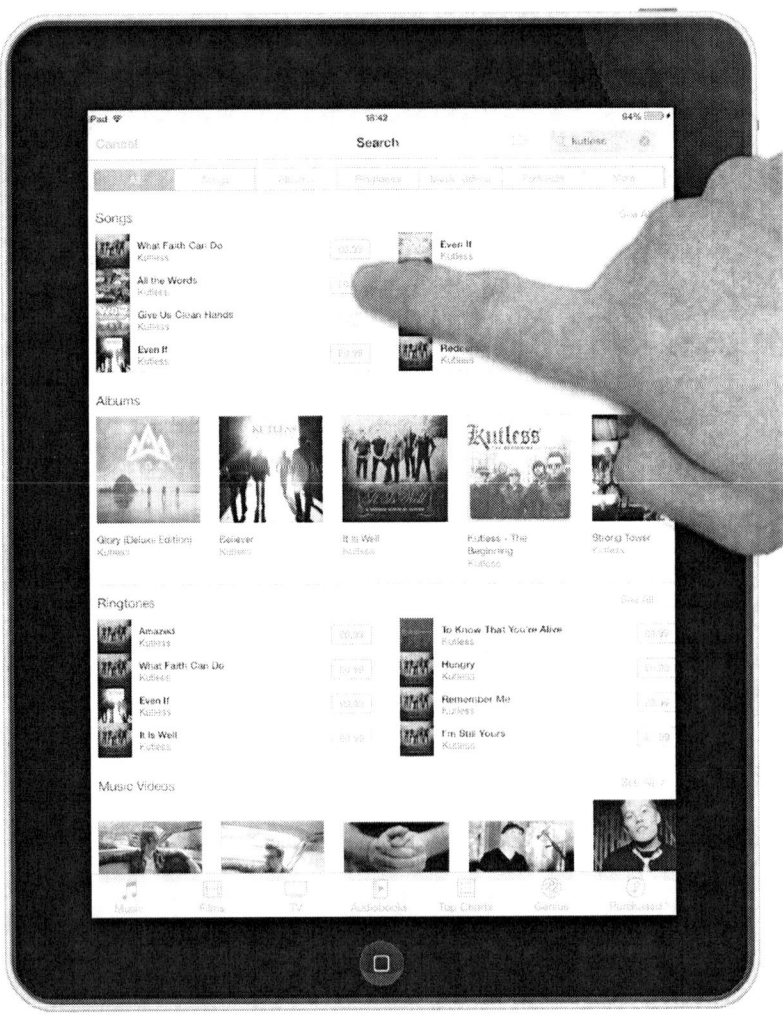

To buy any of the tracks or albums, tap your finger on the price tag.

You will need your apple id to buy any of the media.

Chapter 3: Using your iPad

Transferring Music from your Computer

To get music onto iPad you can purchase and download from the iTunes Store or sync with iTunes on your computer, by connecting your iPad using the iPad cable.

Open iTunes on your computer and click the iPad icon on the top right of the tool bar

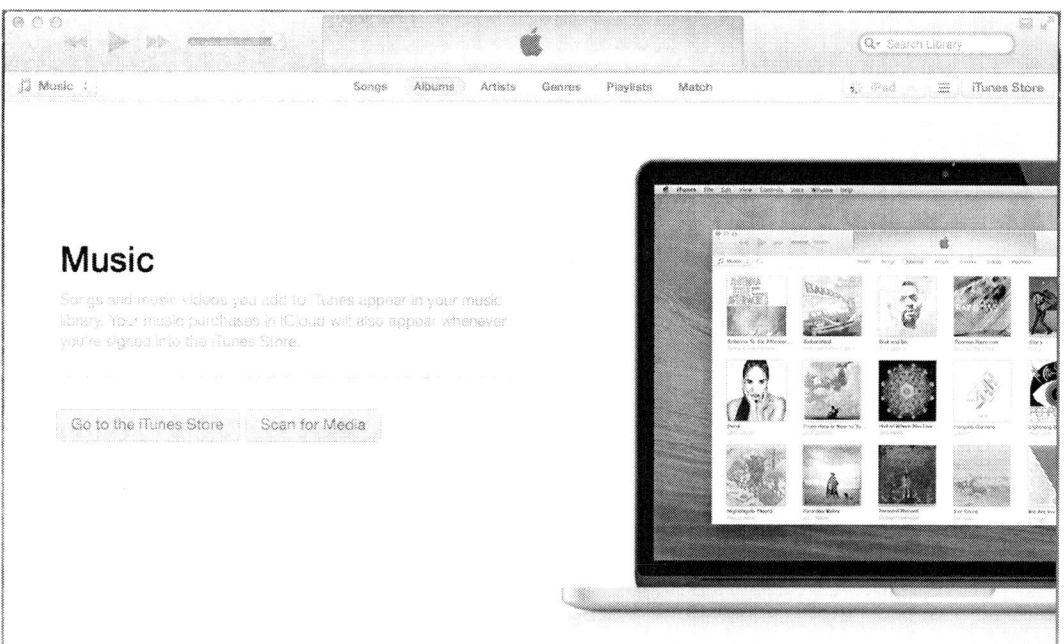

iTunes on a Mac showing connected iPad

Chapter 3: Using your iPad

Below is a summary of the iPad that has been connected to the computer.

Scroll down to the bottom of this page and select 'manually manage music and videos'. This allows you to select the songs or albums you want to transfer instead of syncing your whole library.

Once you have done that, enable your sidebar in iTunes. I find this helps when transferring songs or albums to an iPad

Chapter 3: Using your iPad

You can do this by going to the view menu and selecting show sidebar.

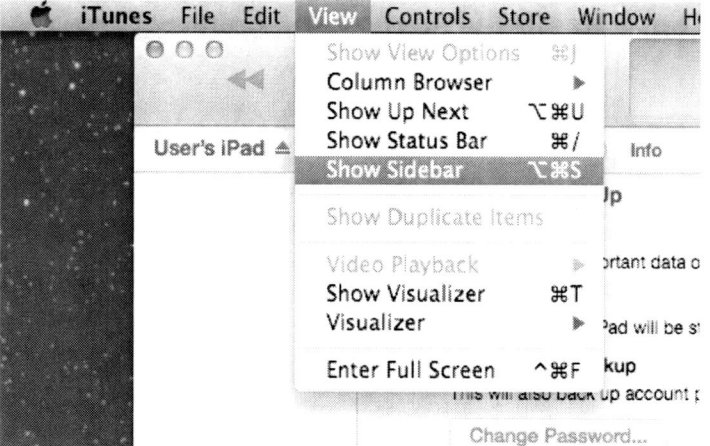

Now select your music library from the top left.

To add any music to your iPad, just drag and drop the track or album onto the iPad device shown in the left hand sidebar.

Chapter 3: Using your iPad

Taking Notes

To start notes app, tap on the icon on the home screen

When notes has loaded you can view your current notes alone the left hand side or add a new note by tapping the pen on the top right.

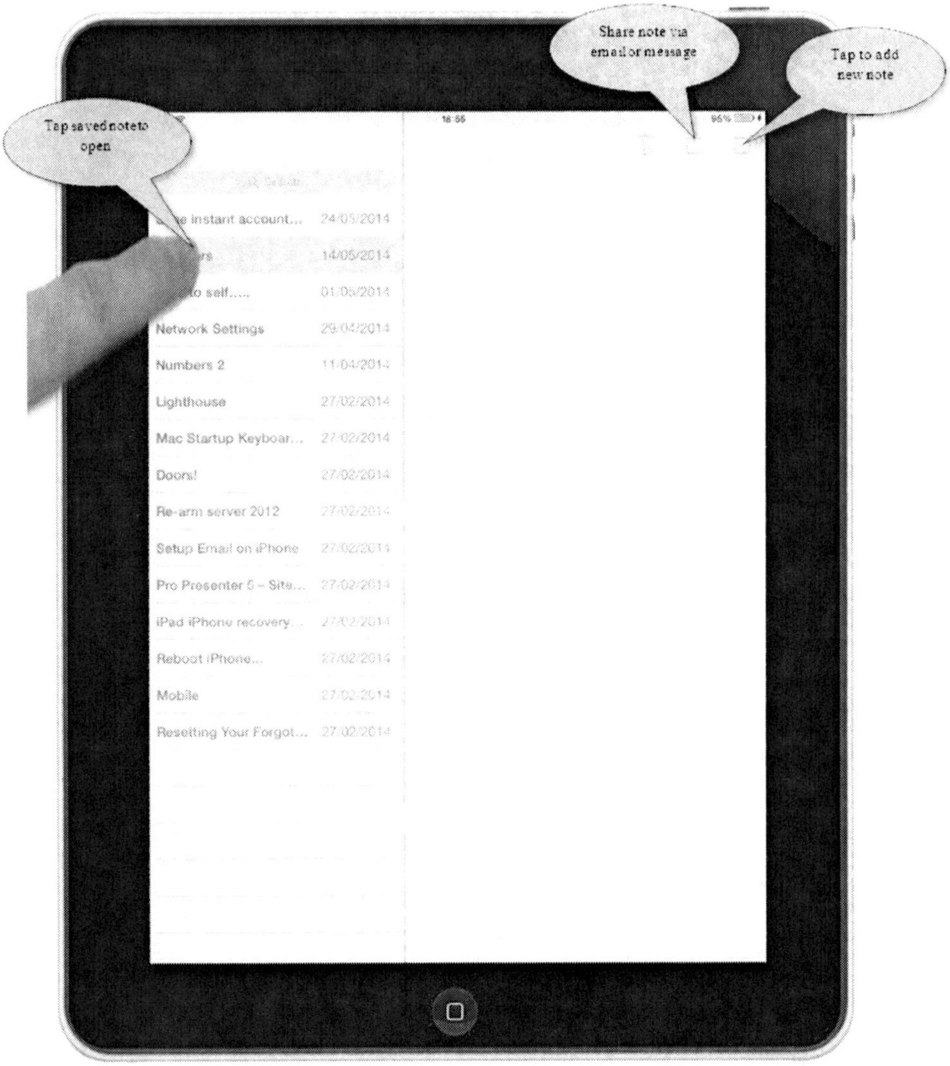

Chapter 3: Using your iPad

Reminders

To start reminders app, tap on the icon on the home screen

To add reminders, tap reminders then on a blank line on the paper

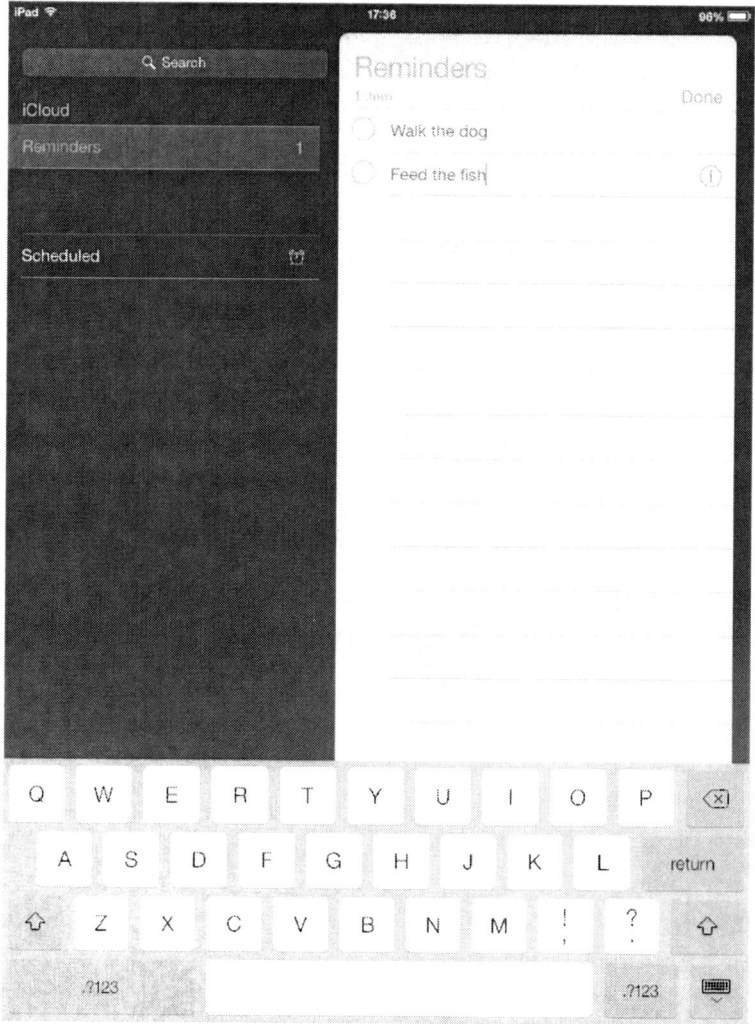

Tap return to add another reminder.

These are reminders of things to do today.

65

Chapter 3: Using your iPad

To schedule reminders, tap scheduled on the left hand side of the screen

Add a reminder by tapping on a blank line and entering a description of the task.

Then tap the 'i' icon on the right hand side of the reminder

This will allow you to enter the date and time. Tap 'alarm' then swipe up and down the days and times that appear, shown below.

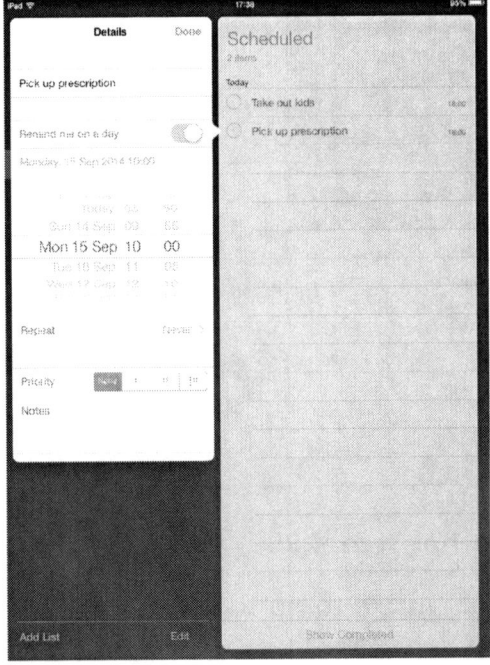

Chapter 3: Using your iPad

FaceTime

To use FaceTime, tap the icon on the home screen. You will need your Apple ID and a Wi-Fi connection to the Internet.

When you open FaceTime, you will be prompted to sign in if you haven't already done so. Once FaceTime has loaded, click on your contacts, you can add friends who have apple ids to your contact list

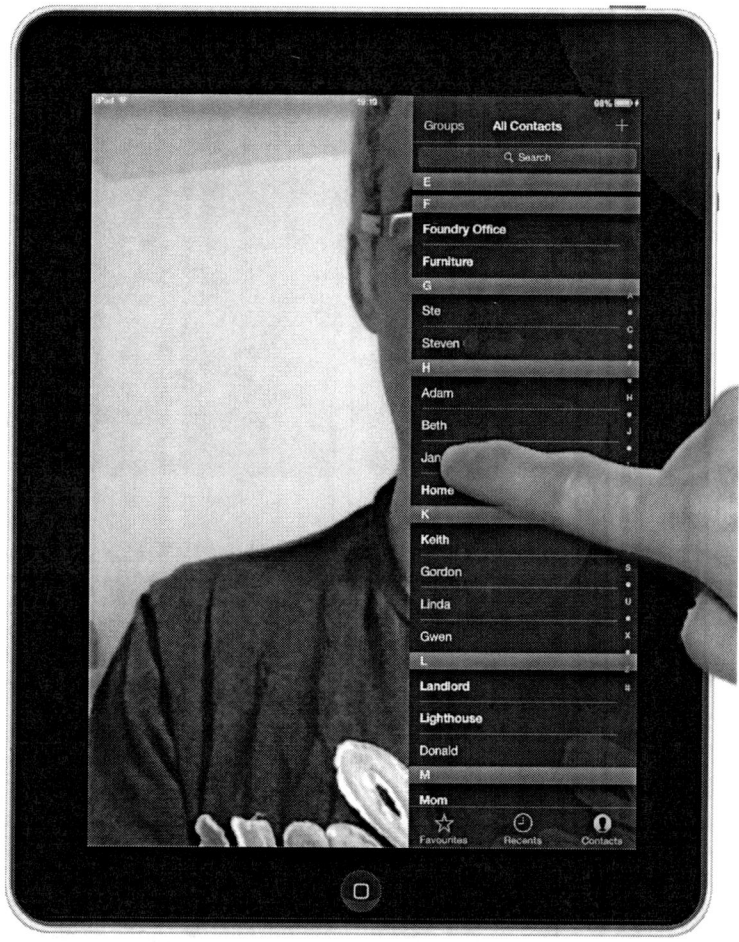

To give them a call, just tap on their name in the contacts list.

Chapter 3: Using your iPad

Then tap on the FaceTime icon shown below.

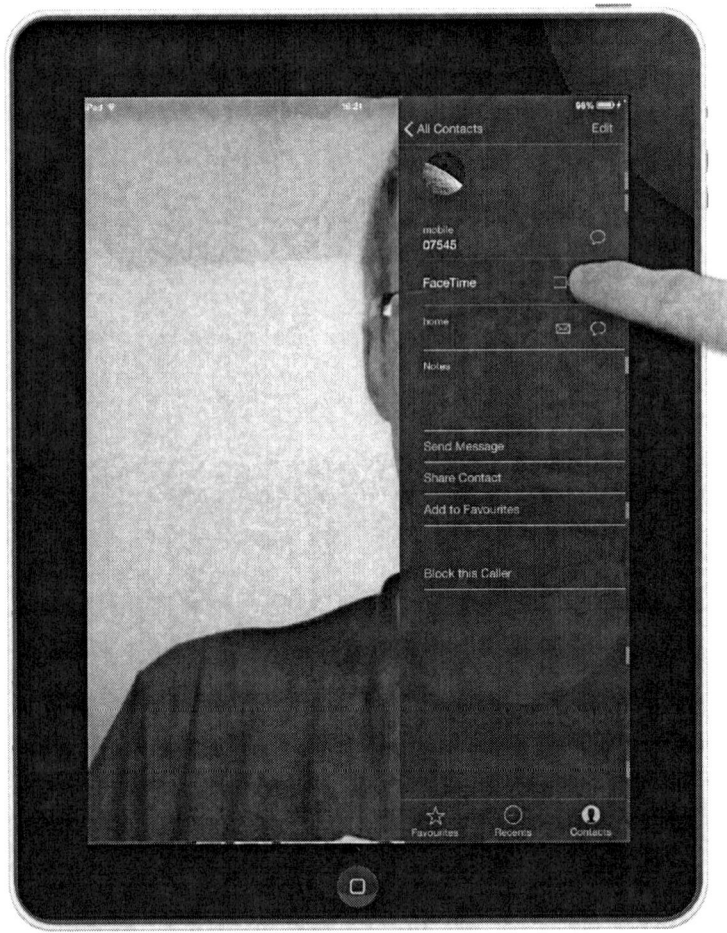

Here you can have a video converstation with them

Chapter 3: Using your iPad

To add a contact click the + icon on the top right of the contacts list.

Add their name and apple id, email or number they use for their facetime.

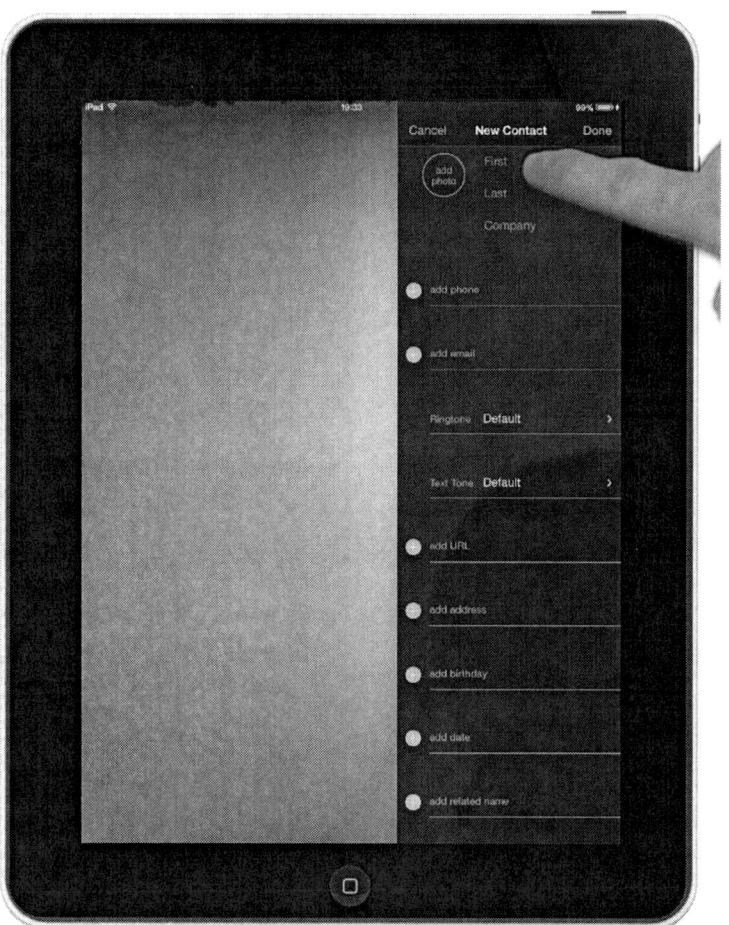

Chapter 3: Using your iPad

Taking Pictures

Tap the camera icon on the home screen.

Now you can use the iPad as you would a digital camera

Chapter 3: Using your iPad

Along the bottom of your screen you can select the type of video or photo you want to take: time lapse, slomo, video, photo, square photo and panoramic photo. You can select them by swiping your finger over them.

Once you have taken your photo you can you can crop or rotate the image

To crop the image, use the grid shown above to highlight the section of the photograph you want to keep.

You can adjust a photograph by rotating it slightly by dragging the dials up and down as shown above left. This helps with straightening images that were not taken very straight.

71

Chapter 3: Using your iPad

You can also change the shading and tonal effects of the image, making your image black and white, a sepia effect or boost the colours by tapping on the icon highlighted below and tapping on an effect

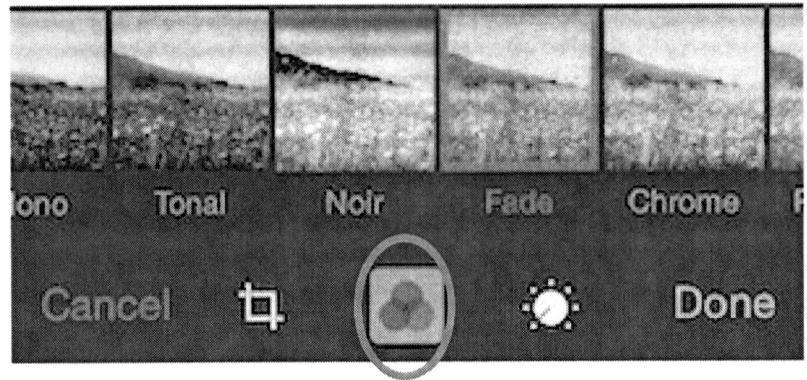

You can adjust the brightness and contrast or highlight shadows where photographs have come out dark in places.

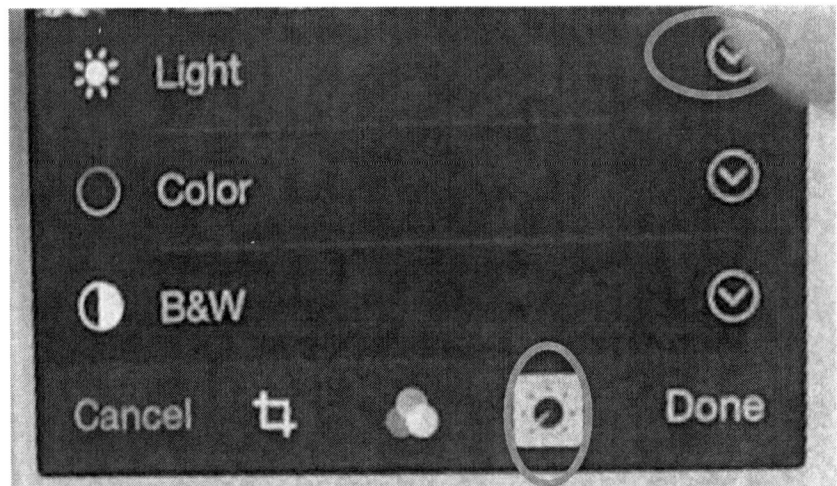

You can do this by tapping on the adjust icon circled above then from the menu, tap the down arrow on the right hand side to open up the options, select from exposure, highlights, shadows, brightness, contrast and blackpoint to change the brightness, contrast, highlight shadows etc.

Chapter 3: Using your iPad

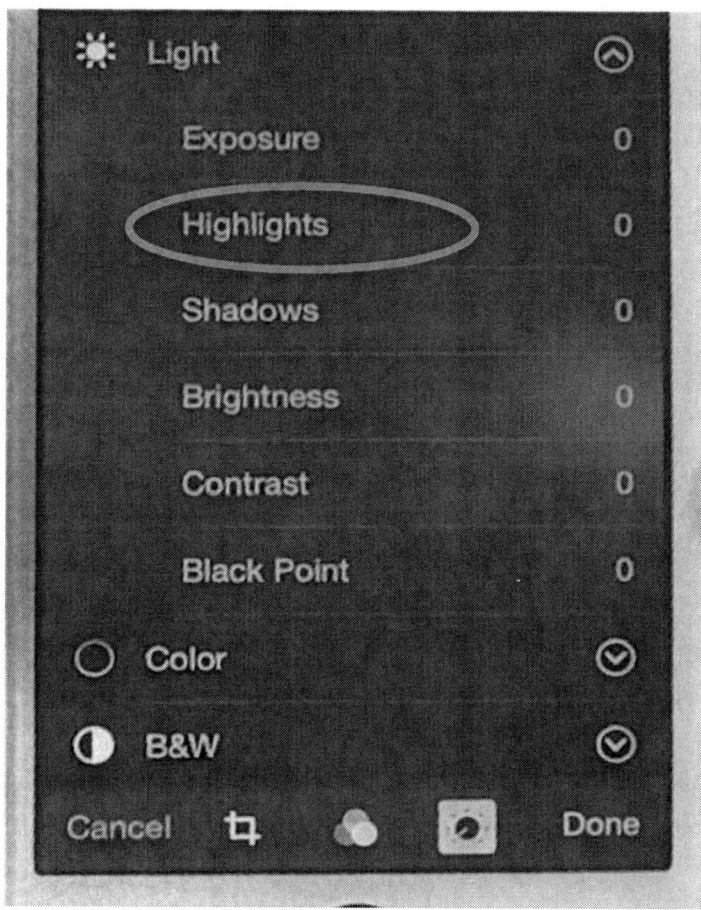

Tap on highlights to lighten some of the dark shadows in your image, etc

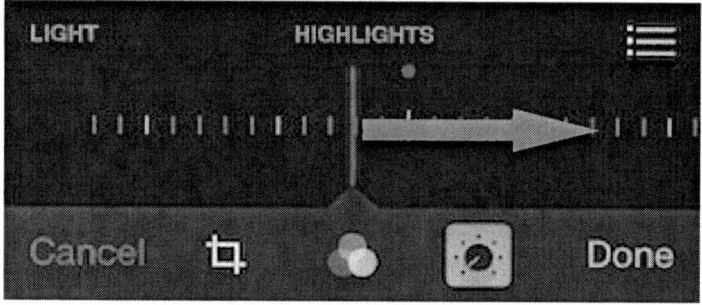

Drag the bar left and right to change the highlight

Chapter 3: Using your iPad

Siri

Siri is an extremely useful feature. It allows you to talk to your iPad, sometimes referred to as a virtual assistant; it can help you with all kinds of things. You can use Siri to send messages, schedule meetings, and search for nearby restaurants all without having to type a single letter.

To use Siri, just press and hold the Home button on your device. Then tell Siri what you need.

Try saying: "Send email to" (pick a name from your contacts list)

Try saying: "What is the weather like tomorrow"

Try saying: "Find me a website on baking a cake"

The more you use Siri, the better it will understand you as it will grow accustomed to your voice.

Chapter 3: Using your iPad

Voice Dictation

Another useful feature of Siri is voice dictation, which allows you to enter text without having to use the keyboard. You can search the web, take notes, post an update to Facebook, and more just by speaking.

To use voice dictation, tap the microphone icon on your on screen keyboard. Then start dictating the text you want Siri to type. It listens to what you say, and types it. The more you use it the better Siri gets at understanding you.

You can even add punctuation by saying words like "period" or 2 "question mark" when you reach the end of a sentence.

Chapter 3: Using your iPad

Arranging Icons

On your home screen tap and hold your finger on one of the icons.

This means you can move icons around the screen or onto the next page. To move an icon tap and hold your finger on an icon then move your finger to drag the icon.

For icons you use the most, you can drag them to your dock at the bottom.

Chapter 3: Using your iPad

You can get to the other pages by swiping your finger left and right to turn the page

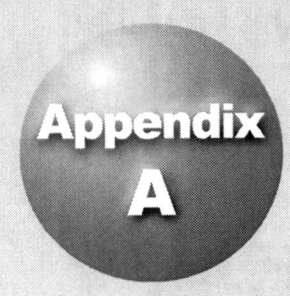

Installing iOS 8

Both the iPhone 6 and iPhone 6 Plus will ship with iOS 8.

Apple usually limits system updates to its newer devices.

iPhone 4S,

iPhone 5,

iPhone 5C,

iPhone 5S,

iPod touch 5th generation,

iPad 2, iPad 3, iPad 4, iPad Air and iPad Mini.

Before upgrading, make sure you have some time where you don't need to use your iPhone or iPad as it will be temporarily inoperative while the installation takes place.

Appendix A: Installing iOS 8

Backup everything on your iPhone/iPad.

If you use iCloud for your backups, go to Settings, iCloud, Storage and Backup, then tap 'Back Up Now',

If you use iTunes to do so. Plug in your device, click your device on sidebar on iTunes, and select 'Back Up Now'. A backup will then be saved onto your computer's hard disk.

On your iPad go to Software Update option in Settings.

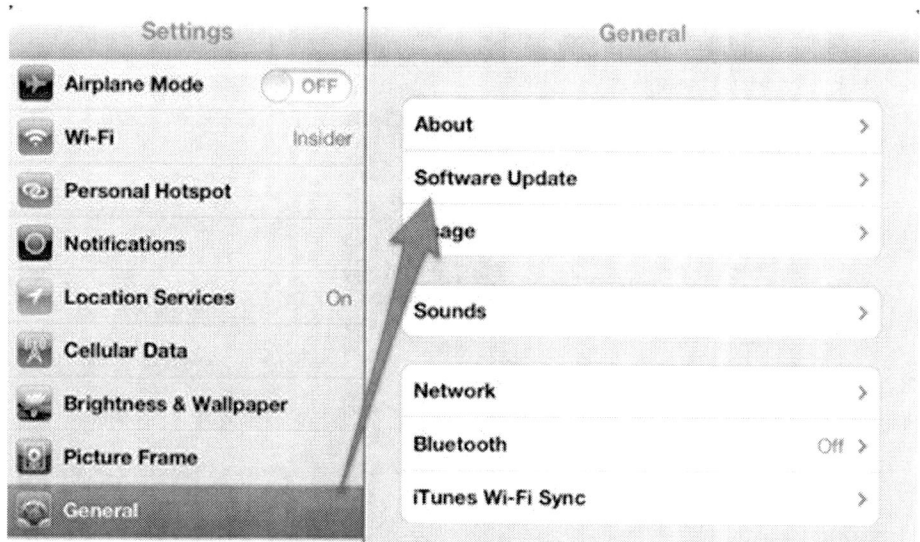

Make sure your device is connected to both Wi-Fi and a power supply, then tap Download and Install to do so.

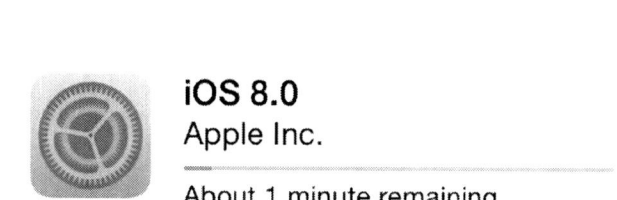

Depending on your internet connection the installation might take a while.

Appendix A: Installing iOS 8

If you prefer to update using iTunes,

Connect your iPad using the cable to a USB port and select your device from the sidebar under devices.

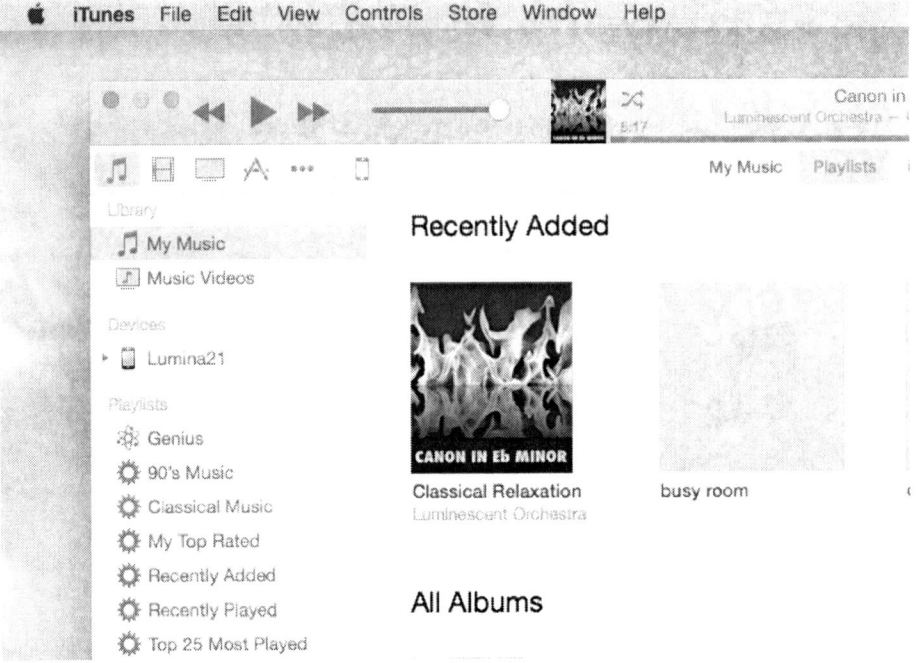

Under Summary, click Check for Update, then choose Download and Install, and it should be taken care of.

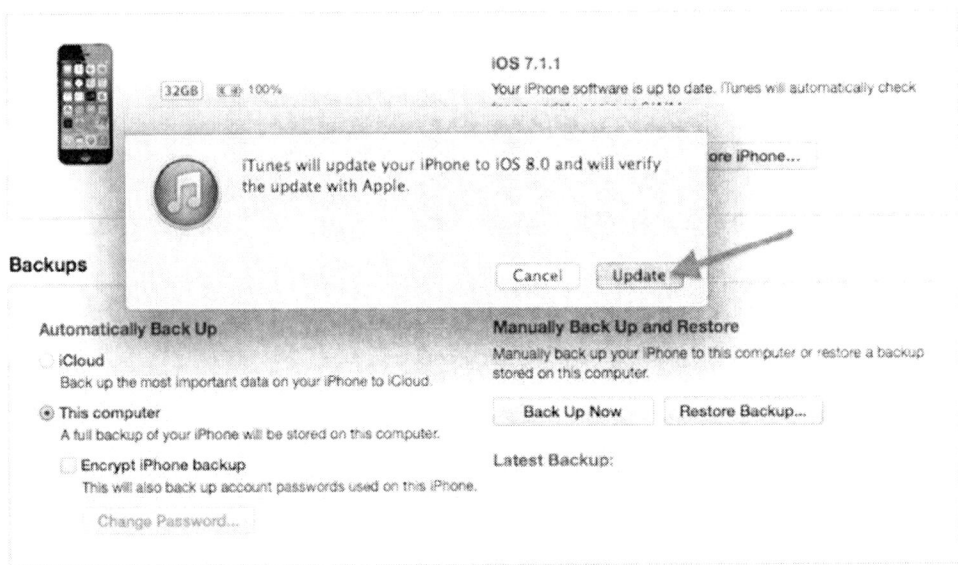

Confirm your iCloud details and start using your phone

Appendix A: Installing iOS 8

When the update is complete, your device should restart automatically. Once it does, you may be asked to enter some iCloud details, and set security questions. After these have been filled out, your newly updated device should be ready to use.

Appendix B: iOS 8 Settings

You can access the settings by tapping on the settings icon on the home screen

Here you can change system settings, personal preferences etc for the different apps and functions of your iPad

Appendix B: iOS 8 Settings

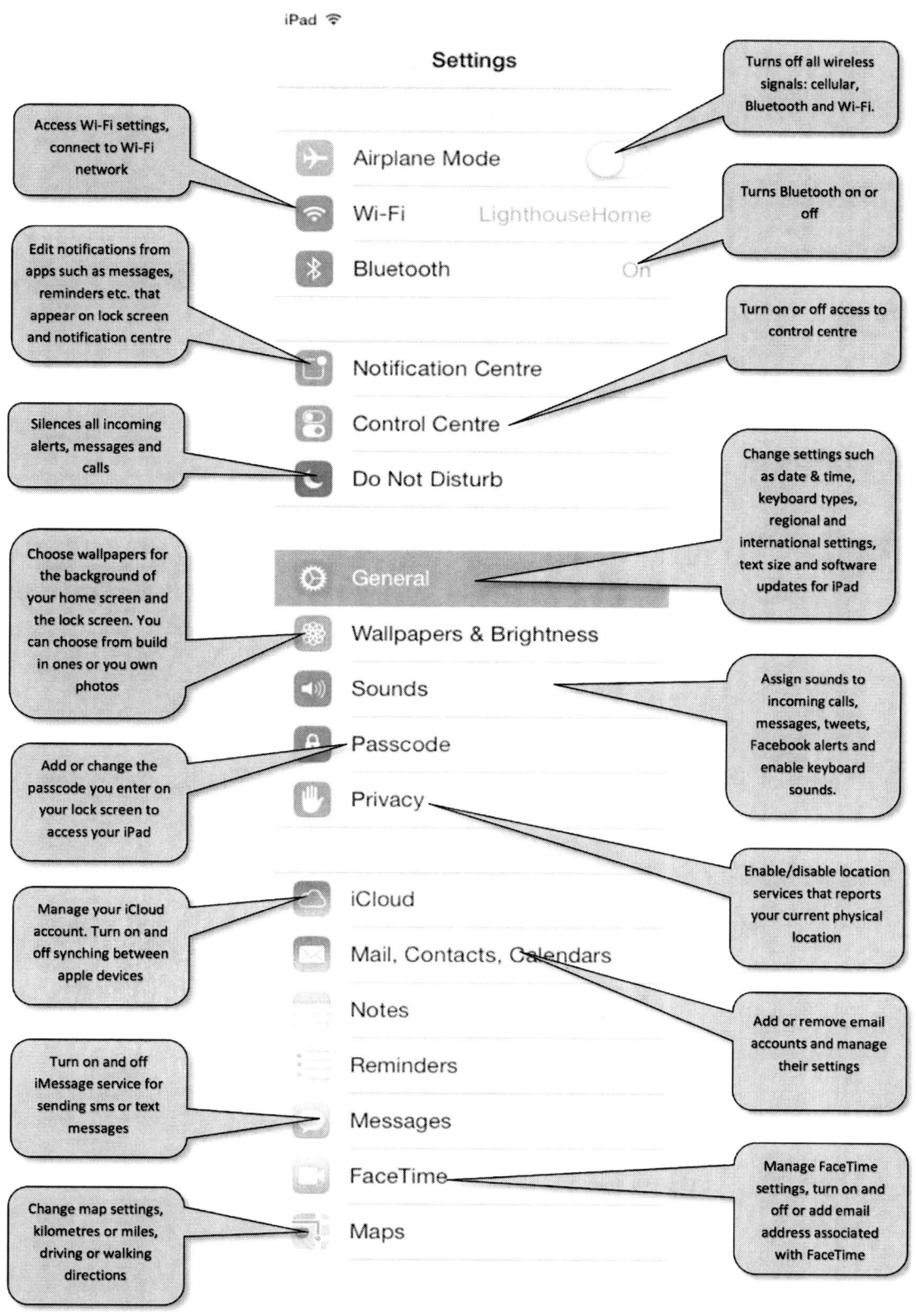

83

Appendix B: iOS 8 Settings

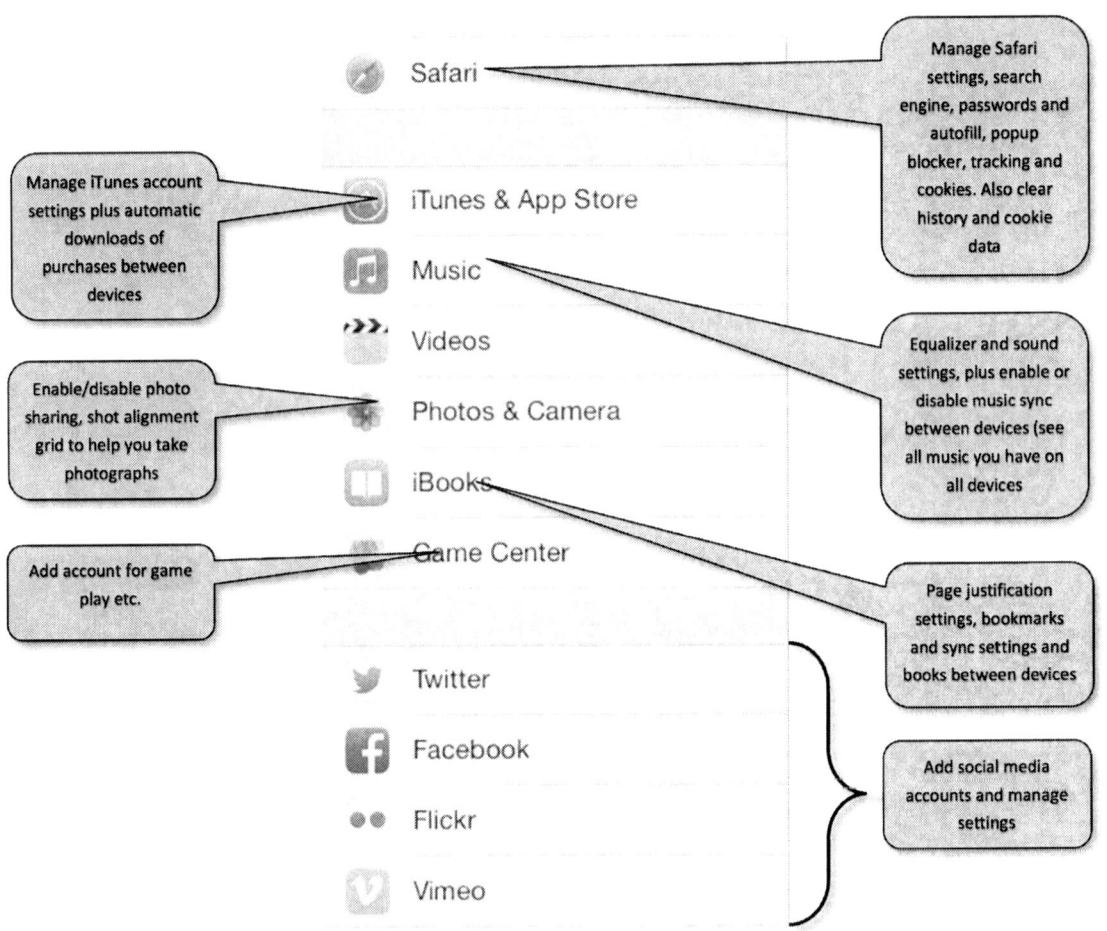

Appendix B: iOS 8 Settings

My Notes & Settings

Here is a section for you to write down all your settings, notes and keep them in a safe place.

However, be careful what settings you write down, if you write down passwords or credit card info make sure the book is kept safe. It is safer not to write this info down.

All other information such as email addresses account settings, technical settings etc are safe to write down.

Appendix C: My Notes & Settings

Appendix C: My Notes & Settings

Appendix C: My Notes & Settings

Appendix C: My Notes & Settings

Appendix C: My Notes & Settings

Appendix C: My Notes & Settings

Appendix C: My Notes & Settings

Appendix C: My Notes & Settings

Appendix C: My Notes & Settings

Appendix C: My Notes & Settings

Appendix C: My Notes & Settings

Appendix C: My Notes & Settings

Appendix C: My Notes & Settings

Appendix C: My Notes & Settings

Appendix C: My Notes & Settings

CPSIA information can be obtained at www.ICGtesting.com
Printed in the USA
LVOW09s1407301114

416285LV00020B/704/P